LONDON TRAMWAY TWILIGHT

1949–1952

ROBERT J HARLEY

Capital Transport

I dedicate this book to the memory of Roy Hubble. His love of London's tramways was an inspiration to others.

ISBN 185414 234 8
Published by Capital Transport Publishing
38 Long Elmes, Harrow Weald, Middlesex
Printed by CS Graphics, Singapore
Designed by Tim Demuth
© Robert J Harley 2000

Title page An animated scene at the corner of McLeod Road and Knee Hill, Abbey Wood, is played out in bright sunshine. Standard E/1 car 1533 follows ex-West Ham car 344 towards the terminus. A 698 trolleybus has also squeezed into the view. In those days Abbey Wood was served exclusively by electric traction. Capital Transport

Right Dusk has faded into evening in this quintessential view of a tram on the Victoria Embankment. This image of an era long ago will evoke a wealth of memories for many readers. One can almost sense the chill in the air, the sound of the Thames gently lapping on the river bank and the rustle of the bare branches – all sensations that complement the reassuring presence of the tramcar, which will take Londoners safely to the end of the line. Capital Transport collection

CONTENTS

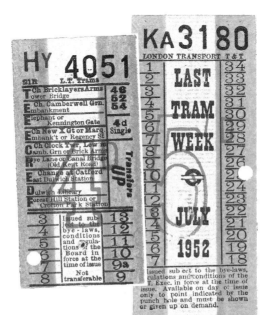

Above A pair of trams on Docklands routes 68 and 70 are depicted at the Greenwich terminus in Church Street. Various London Transport officials seem to be in a debate as to the next course of action. Whatever the outcome, one presumes that car 554 (if not suffering from mechanical failure) will quickly reverse past the waiting 68 to return to London Bridge, Tooley Street. Capital Transport

Right What better way for a family to travel to town than by tramcar? Here on the Embankment several youngsters are being taken out to enjoy the springtime sights. Car 1907 has a more prosaic task ahead of it, as it journeys back through the streets of South London. Capital Transport

Facing page A poignant reminder of the maxim that 'all things must pass' is provided by car 1931, which is standing in Woolwich New Road during the last week of operation. This particular tram would later be one of the very last cars to run on London's first generation tramway system. Capital Transport

INTRODUCTION
AND ACKNOWLEDGEMENTS

THE GREATEST pleasure in writing this book has been to bring to life a past era – a time when a small boy could stand at a tram stop on Well Hall Road and wonder at the seemingly endless procession of red tramcars. It is fair to say that no other public transport vehicle serving the capital has aroused so much passion and controversy.

First and foremost, I want to present to the reader a 'People's History' of the last years of the London tramways, and with this in mind I have avoided paraphrasing, but rather let witnesses speak in their own words. Reminiscences included in this book have flowed from the pens of Dr Gerald Druce, Father Benedict Sankey OSB, Alan Watkins, Julian Thompson, Dr John Chambers, Roy Hubble, John Price and a number of unnamed reporters who filed copy with South London newspapers. Many friends have willingly given of their time and expertise to assist in this project, and without them the text could not have been written. My particular thanks go to the trio of Croydonians – John Meredith, John Gent and B. 'Curly' Cross.

Julian Thompson very nobly sent a vast array of newspaper cuttings plus extracts from his tramway diaries and these form the basis of many day to day events recorded in the text. Another stalwart was John Barrie who, with the assistance of John Wills, combed personal archives to supply many relevant details of fleet allocation and crew conditions. On the latter topic, David Profit has given me first hand information on the life of a tram conductor. I acknowledge my debt to all the photographers who have kindly made their collections available for publication; especially I would like to thank Alan Cross and Clarence Carter. I am grateful for Terry Russell's expertise in supplying detailed car plans. A significant note of gratitude goes to Dave Jones, who cheerfully put up with all my requests for extra resources from the extensive LCC Tramways Trust collections. The Trust now administers the photographic work of Messrs Thompson, Hubble, Mackenzie, Battams and Rayfield. I also wish to thank Ken Glazier and Gerald Druce who have studied the text and have suggested alterations and improvements. To satisfy those readers who desire further background knowledge, I have

included a selective bibliography at the end of this book. I would like to acknowledge the expertise of my good friend Ashley Best in preparing the cover painting.

One of my main aims has been to appeal to younger readers, who can now experience a new tramway culture in South London, very different from the one which existed in the years 1949 to 1952. I sincerely hope they will use this book as a reference point for their history and local environmental studies coursework. To this end I have given most measurements with metric equivalents, and would inform those too young to remember, that £1 was once composed of twenty shillings, each shilling having twelve pence. I have also tried to explain pre-decimal money in terms of its purchasing power in the early post-war years.

Finally, any mistakes in the text are my own, but I trust they will not detract from the reader's enjoyment of the whole saga of the last few years of London's first generation tramway system.

LONDON'S TRAMWAY INHERITANCE

HE FINAL few years of the London tramways represent the culmination of a long series of events. This process cannot be understood in isolation and it is helpful to study the evolution of the system, and the turns of history which brought about its downfall.

The story of passenger carrying tramways in the capital begins on 23rd March 1861, when George Francis Train opened his Bayswater Road horse car line, and ends on 5th July 1952, when the last electric trams were replaced by diesel buses. In the intervening ninety-one years tramways played an important part in the life of the metropolis. Routes were provided in the most populous areas, where cheap fares and frequent services enabled large numbers of people to achieve greater mobility. Many of London's poorer citizens could now live further from their place of work; for a few pennies they and their families could also reach the fresh air and green fields of the suburbs. However, there were always those in society who feared any upsurge of the working classes; many 'carriage' folk showed a dogged animosity towards tramways which they imagined would lower property values and generally damage well-to-do neighbourhoods. These reactionary attitudes manifested themselves in the refusal of several inner London local authorities and the City of London to allow any tramway presence along many prestigious thoroughfares.

The situation of London's horse tramways in 1875 reflected the divisions in contemporary social order. A network of lines belonging to the North Metropolitan Company stretched from Holloway to Stratford in the east. The hallowed ground of the City of London was not served and passengers had to walk from either Finsbury Square or Aldgate. Nor were any horse cars permitted to traverse the London bridges. Thus, tramlines south of the River Thames had termini at the foot of Vauxhall Bridge, Westminster Bridge and Blackfriars Bridge, where connecting routes ran to Clapham,

Brixton, New Cross, Blackheath Hill and Greenwich.

Critics and doubters were not slow in expressing their opinions. In the 1875 edition of *Tramways: Their Construction and Working*, Captain Tyler, R. E., a Government Inspector, sounds a note of warning:

'The comparatively good condition of the road surfaces, the common use of cabs and omnibuses, and the number of these vehicles available for general purposes at reasonable fares, have all combined to render tram rails less necessary here (in central London) than anywhere else. The numbers of private vehicles in use, whose owners naturally look upon tramways with suspicion, if not with absolute dislike, are also greater. Certain vested interests are or have been more or less opposed to tramways; the numerous bodies by whom the streets are owned or maintained are difficult to deal with, with a view to combined permissions for complete tramway routes; and the existing railway and omnibus companies cannot, in many cases, consider tramway companies otherwise than as formidable competitors.'

The irony of these statements was probably not lost on the tramway companies who were obliged by Act of Parliament to maintain a width of roadway amounting to almost eight feet for every single track tramway. It can truly be said that they paved the way for

their bus competitors and every other highway user on wheels.

Central London was bus territory, and the London General Omnibus Company exploited this advantage to the full. The other serious competitor to the tramways was the steadily growing system of underground and tube railways which was greatly expanded from the 1890s onwards.

The tramway companies persevered and by 1895 an extension of services had brought the benefits of horse cars to places such as Plumstead, Catford, Tulse Hill, Wandsworth, Kew Bridge, Harlesden Green, Hampstead, Edmonton, Leyton and West Ham. All lines were constructed to standard gauge, with the exception of the Highgate Hill and Woolwich & South East London companies which opted for a narrow gauge of 42ins (1067mm). Developments in mechanical traction included the appearance of cable trams on Highgate Hill and from Brixton to Streatham Hill. Steam trams were also tried between Finsbury Park, Wood Green and Ponders End. The isolated system in Croydon staged experiments with battery operated trams, and indeed, it was to electricity as a source of motive power that the tramway world turned. The speedy development of reliable electric traction in the United States was contemporary with the purchase of most of the capital's company operated tramways by the LCC and neighbouring local authorities. The impetus grew for municipal operators to replace their horse trams. In a report, dated 15th October 1898, J. Allen Baker shares his thoughts with the rest of the London County Council's Highways Committee:

'The question of the best form of traction for London is one of the first importance, as the ever growing congestion of traffic in our streets is a problem that is becoming daily more difficult of solution, and any system that would give a more rapid and economical service and relieve the streets of the many thousands of horses now used to haul our tramcars would provide a public boon.'

All well and good – electric traction gets the green light from the County Council. However, it becomes increasing apparent on reading the report that J. Allen Baker has qualms about recommending the overhead trolley system of current collection. He is favourably impressed by the underground conduit method which he studied in North America. He ends his twenty-nine page report with the following fateful statement:

'It therefore becomes simply a consideration of the difference in first cost between the street construction of the conduit as versus the overhead – a matter perhaps of £1000 to £2000 per mile of track for the cheaper form of conduit, and £2000 to £4000 for a heavier construction similar to that of New York and Washington – and the question whether for so comparatively small a sum any portion of our great city should have anything but the best system obtainable. Provincial cities with their wider and less busy streets and comparatively small populations, may find it to their interest to adopt the cheaper overhead construction, and tramway companies will naturally always prefer the cheaper form where they can obtain municipal sanction to instal it. But London, with its endless population, its unprecedentedly busy streets and congested traffic, need not hesitate to adopt the system that will give the greatest satisfaction to the public and the local authorities through whose districts the lines may pass; and of all the systems now before us for consideration, the one in my judgement best suited to the requirements of London is the electric conduit.'

The LCC would eventually rue the day it accepted this report, because there was never to be a 'cheaper form of conduit', in fact the very opposite. The installation and maintenance of miles of conduit tramway throughout the LCC area would always constitute a major drain on financial resources. London employed a centre slot system, and current was collected by a detachable plough held in a carrier under each tram. All in all, around 123 route miles (197kms) were equipped with conduit, and the expense of construction, on a per mile of route basis, was just over twice that for a conventional overhead wire tramway.

Unfortunately, the conduit system exhibited many shortcomings. Track joints often worked loose and plough fractures were a significant source of breakdowns, frequently causing unnecessary delays. The conduit also amplified sound especially within the confines of the Kingsway Subway.

Needless to say, every other tramway operator in the metropolitan area opted for the cheaper, tried and tested method of overhead wire current collection. Joint working over both systems became a reality when, in November 1908, the first change pit from conduit to overhead was opened. Thereafter, other LCC overhead trolley lines, the Metropolitan Electric Tramways in North London, several East London municipalities, and Croydon participated in through running with tramcars fitted with trolley poles and plough carriers.

Throughout the first decade of the twentieth century electric tramways became a common sight in the metropolitan region. In order to service the LCC network, a new works was constructed at Charlton; this was referred to as the Central Repair Depot, or CRD for short. However, progress was severely limited in providing tram routes

Right Trams still performed vast crowd moving feats even into their twilight years. Here in New Cross Road, no less than ten cars edge their way westwards in the direction of New Cross Depot and various inner London termini. The availability of a fixed route transport system also had a psychological effect on potential passengers, and it was a comforting thought that if the tracks were there, a tram would be along in a minute. C.Carter

Facing page A tram on route 44 forks left into Grand Depot Road, whilst Car 1914 on route 72 reaches the top of Woolwich New Road. There were several sections in London where tracks took different streets on a one way basis. This location is situated on the edge of the valley of the Thames, and it was prone to swirling mists which caused restricted visibility. At such times cars would descend Grand Depot Road hill very gingerly, trying to avoid a slow speed encounter with a tram in front which had stopped to let a passenger off. R. Hubble

across the West End and the Cities of London and Westminster. In 1906 the LCC did succeed in opening the first stage of the Kingsway Subway – a pioneer cross-London transport facility linking the northern and southern halves of the LCC network. It might have been assumed that since the subway was out-of-sight of the objectors, that the way forward was obvious. Not a bit of it! The LCC still failed to gain permission for other through routes, some of which would have used sub-surface tunnels. Construction of new tramways was now a political issue, both in the national sense with the Liberals confronting the Conservatives, and in the purely local arena with the Progressives and Moderates vying for control of the LCC.

In spite of all these setbacks, large numbers of passengers were transported and electric tramway connections bound together many communities, particularly those thickly populated areas of East and South London, where cheap workmen's fares were vital to the functioning of the docks and many other engineering industries.

The heyday of the London tram was probably before the First World War, and in 1911 alone, trams carried two-thirds of the total passengers in Greater London. When the war did come in 1914, government agencies praised the way the tramways handled crowds of workers to the Woolwich Arsenal and other vital munitions establishments.

A chill wind of economics began to blow in the 1920s. By 1921 trams carried one half of London's passengers; by 1927 this figure had dropped to one third. Wage and material costs rose steadily. Outdated rolling stock had to be replaced or renovated. Already one of London's company owned tramways, the London United, had to go cap in hand to the London County Council for loans to keep track and vehicles operating safely. To add insult to injury, bus competition began to make serious inroads into tramway revenues, and bus companies were not slow in advertising through services past tram termini into the more select shopping areas of the West End. It was now only a matter of time before the first casualty, and not surprisingly the vulnerable LUT, which started out in 1901 as Sir James Clifton Robinson's grand creation with a large fleet housed in the spacious Fulwell Depot, felt compelled to axe its Richmond Bridge to Twickenham route in October 1924. London General bus route 27 supplanted the rail bound vehicles.

More bad news was on the horizon, and on 28th March 1927 a small knot of well-wishers gathered outside East Croydon Station for the valedictory celebrations of the George Street to Addiscombe service which was about to be replaced by bus route 178. In the same year as the Addiscombe conversion, in the semi-official book *London Rebuilt 1897–1927*, author Harold Clunn remarks:

'While London as a whole has never been very partial to the tramways as a means of getting about, the prejudice which was shown against them some twenty years ago is more justified at the present day, owing to the great improvement in the motor omnibuses, and the advantages of the free wheel traffic, compared with the fixed wheel or rail system of locomotion.'

Clunn goes on to describe the 'startling postwar developments' in the provision of housing in vast new estates. Becontree is cited with its 'wide and well planned roads and pleasant houses amidst spacious gardens' – all ripe territory for the motor bus operators. But even in adversity, the tramcar did attempt to retain its role, and several operators introduced new vehicles, the most remarkable of which were the 100 type UCC or Feltham trams which appeared on the roads in 1931. These ultra-modern cars were a revelation and passenger levels on the routes worked by Felthams rose accordingly. They were designed to be the first part of a tramway revival programme for London, whereby new reserved tracks and a shorter version of the Feltham, designed to negotiate sharper curves, were projected.

The LCC was also prompted to construct a sample car, No. 1, intended as the forerunner of a new and improved fleet. In fact the LCC was not only looking to improve its rolling stock, but also it was planning extensions into areas of new council housing.

For many, Car 1 represented the last word in tramway travel. Placed in service in 1932, it is pictured in LT red and cream livery within the confines of Holloway Depot. Unfortunately it was the swansong of the LCC and the idea of producing a batch of similar trams was quickly dropped by the London Passenger Transport Board.

Car 592 has the expanse of Westhorne Avenue, Eltham, to itself. Road, tramway and housing estate were built new in the early 1930s, but no provision was made for reserved tracks. A conventional street tramway was still the order of the day for the conservative minded LCC planners. The bridge in the background carries the Southern Electric suburban railway from Charing Cross to Eltham Well Hall and Dartford. D.A.Thompson

Estates were linked to track extensions in the Downham, Grove Park and Eltham areas. These new routes might have been more effective had the rails been placed on reserved tracks, then currently in vogue with several provincial cities, such as Birmingham and Liverpool. But the LCC opted for conservatism and tramways along Downham Way and Westhorne Avenue were constructed as street track with overhead wires; conduit equipped routes were now so expensive that they were out of the question. Even this brief tramway renaissance was haunted by track abandonments elsewhere, when in 1929 the nearest unconnected system to London, in the north Kent town of Gravesend, succumbed to buses. Two years later in 1931 the LUT started converting its

Kingston area services to trolleybus operation. Worse was to follow in the 1931 Royal Commission report, *The Co-ordination and Development of Transport*. This stated:

'Tramways, if not an obsolete form of transport, are at all events in a state of obsolescence, and cause much unnecessary congestion and considerable danger to the public. We recommend, therefore, (a) that no additional tramways should be constructed, and (b) that, though no definite time limit can be laid down, they should gradually disappear and give place to other forms of transport.'

Of course, these findings could be hotly disputed. Tramway travel was inherently safe, the tramcars themselves were solidly built and average speeds were low. However, the increase in private motoring resulted in a number of fatal accidents where passengers attempting to board trams were knocked down in the street. The fact that this problem could have been alleviated by provision of loading islands, seems to have escaped the notice of the commission, who seemed not to have considered seriously any foreign 'best practice' in the advice to Parliament.

Although the report was flawed, it is fair to assume that the planners of the 1930s accepted the recommendations on face value. Even without this establishment 'thumbs down', all tramway progress was effectively halted in July 1933 by the compulsory integration of the capital's public transport into the London Passenger Transport Board. The seventeen tramway operators in the capital contributed some 2,600 cars running over 327 route miles (523km). Trams still accounted for thirty percent of the LPTB's passenger journeys. It became apparent that from 1933 onwards the writing was well and truly on the wall for the tramways, and the energies of the new board (known to all as London Transport) were devoted to promoting the trolleybus as the new wonder alternative to the outdated tramcar. The only glimmer of hope rested in the fact that in the very early days of the Board it seemed the success of the Felthams might prompt a tramway revival. Statements coming from the LPTB seemed to imply that certain sections of track would be converted to trolleybuses, but trunk routes were to be upgraded to make London's tramways comparable with the 'best in the world'. Sadly these sentiments never achieved reality, and the anti-tram lobby gained the upper hand.

Early conversions were on a small scale, and routes serving Haydons Road, Wimbledon and the local service from Dartford to Wilmington were given over to motor bus operation. The publicity machine at 55 Broadway, headquarters of the LPTB, was

well aware that press coverage of the trolleybuses produced a very favourable reaction. From the summer of 1935 onwards the general public was invited to enjoy the luxury of new vehicles which had none of the faults of the old trams they were replacing. Trams which in many cases retained hard wooden seats and open top decks.

At the dawn of the London Transport era the first official report confirmed a total of 2,560 trams operating over 327 route miles, with a further five miles of route authorised, but not open for traffic. This last statement refers to connections from Walthamstow to Tottenham, and from Grove Park to Eltham, which, not unsurprisingly, remained on the drawing board, although the former link eventually became part of the trolleybus system. Subsequent London Transport reports make increasingly depressing reading for tramway supporters, and for the year ended 30th June 1939 the route mileage was down to 135, and the fleet had contracted to 1,316 cars, whilst the number of trolleybuses had shot up to 1,411 vehicles.

A brief respite came in 1935–37 when the new board reconditioned a number of trams. These 'rehab' cars, as they were known in tramway circles, benefited from renovated bodywork, upgraded seating and internal fittings. The disappointing part was that the target of 1,000 vehicles was soon reduced to 250, and in the event only just over 150 trams emerged from the CRD at Charlton in their reconditioned state. A further disappointment was that these reconditioned trams continued to ride on old trucks equipped with magnetic brakes. The opportunity was lost to purchase up-to-date electrical equipment including new trucks and air brakes for every vehicle.

Across London in the Southall works of AEC, and in the confines of LT's own Chiswick Works, another vehicle project would soon come to fruition in the appearance of RT 1. This bus was unveiled to the public in July 1939 and it would be the first of a vast fleet. The future looked grim for the tramcar, and already vague hints were being made about the 'transitory' nature of the trolleybus. Electric street traction had met its nemesis.

Aside from the deteriorating political situation in Europe, there were other straws in the wind that would have confirmed or bolstered LT's tram scrapping decision. In Britain large cities such as Manchester and Birmingham had already commenced the transition to buses and trolleybuses. Abroad, the comprehensive network which once served Paris had completely disappeared by 1938. In the United States tramway mileage had fallen considerably throughout the 1920s and 1930s.

Above 'Rehab' or reconditioned cars were a common sight on the postwar system. They really represented only a half hearted attempt to modernise the fleet, and many, particularly those with only one trolley pole, went to the scrap heap before their unrebuilt sisters. Car 1381 was rehabilitated in December 1935 and was burnt in March 1951. D.Battams

Below Hampstead Depot was used to store the strategic reserve fleet during the Second World War. In this 1945 view there is evidence of fire damage to the tram on the extreme right. The pit in front is for the traverser which shunted cars sideways around the depot. Note also the standard E/1s in pre-war state without vestibules.

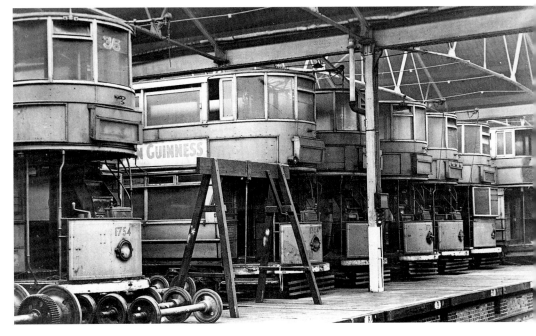

Some of the South London thoroughfares may have been monotonous to those who wanted to traverse the area quickly. However, as we can see at Woolwich Ferry, there is certainly a rich mixture of architecture to distract the eye. Beautiful it certainly isn't, but there is a grim, utilitarian charm about the two power station smoke stacks, the conduit tracks, the trolleybus wiring, the Little Market, run by Beatrice and Nellie Jones and the shanty Corner Snack Bar, where the spoons are chained to the counter!

The start of the Second World War on 3rd September 1939 had a profound effect on London Transport. Trams received 'the blackout treatment' which included blackout masks for headlights, restricted internal lighting and white painted fenders; later, antiblast netting was fixed to the windows. Plans, which included the phasing out of all tramways by 1943, were shelved and everyone got down to the vital task of ensuring the nation's survival. Obviously public transport was crucial; petrol rationing was introduced, private motoring became a luxury of the past and the trams would be retained until the end of hostilities. However, not even Hitler could stop the final conversion of trams north of the Thames, and by Sunday 9th June 1940, only the Kingsway Subway services 31, 33 and 35 remained. This policy attracted some criticism, especially as considerable lengths of still serviceable track, particularly in the East London boroughs, might have been retained for emergency

tram use. As it was, London Transport did halt the tram scrapping programme and a number of surplus vehicles were stored in Hampstead Depot.

South of the river it was business as normal, with a dense network of routes which were now granted an indefinite stay of execution. Although these services were safe from the depredations of London Transport, the Luftwaffe was less merciful, and during the Blitz and the V-bomb campaign of 1944, death and destruction was visited on the tramways. It was said that many folk preferred travelling by tram because the noise of the motors under the lower saloon masked the sound of falling bombs. It was also a comfort to hear the first morning tram after a fraught night in the shelters. Thus the system, worn out as it was, acquired a reputation for reliability and gritty determination to carry the travelling public to victory

In times of great national suffering there were still those engaged on planning London's future, those who had a vision for the capital's postwar rejuvenation. In the 1942 publication, *London Replanned: Interim Report of the Royal Academy Planning Committee*, much emphasis was placed on ring roads with elevated motorways adding to inner city vistas of slab like offices and mass public housing in blocks of flats. Car ownership and frequent bus services, aided by a revamped tube network, were projected to supplement main line railways.

Any lingering hope that the tramways might have a future role was extinguished by the 1943 *County of London Plan* and the 1945 *Greater London Plan*. The former work was commissioned by the LCC, and involved J. H. Forshaw and Professor Patrick Abercrombie in a preparation of a plan for a new London based on predicted future needs. It hardly bears stating that these needs did not include the retention of what was left of the tramway system. One paragraph in the transport section stated that no provision was to be made for tramways, as they were to be superseded by a more modern form of transport. To prove the authors' argument, a photograph purporting to show a traffic jam at the eastern end of Westminster Bridge featured a tramcar stuck in the middle of the chaos – ergo, trams cause congestion – remove the trams and all will be sweetness and light.

What was to replace the remaining trams? Well, the inhabitants of Camberwell were expecting an extension of the Bakerloo tube line to the Green. Other citizens of South London were probably resigned to the fact that trolleybuses would operate over stretches of conduit equipped tramway. This raised the spectacle of overhead wires across Westminster Bridge and along the Victoria Embankment. No-one seemed to know what would eventually happen to the Kingsway Subway, although several fanciful schemes were aired. The tunnel with its restricted clearances was only suitable for railbound traffic, but this did not impede one cheerfully lunatic suggestion in which lowbridge type, double deck diesel buses would work on a one way, single track basis and pass one another at either Holborn or Aldwych stations!

In the event, London Transport devoted five paragraphs in its Annual Report for the year ending 31st December 1946 to the question of tramway abandonment. The section ended with these sentences:

'The certainty of major changes in the traffic flows in London, as a result of railway development and a redistribution of the population as a consequence of planning, makes it essential to select a means of transport not rigidly tied to existing routes. The Board have accordingly decided, with the approval of the Minister of Transport, that fuel oil (diesel) buses shall in due course be substituted for the remaining trams in preference to trolleybuses. This programme will involve the provision of over 1,100 new buses of the latest type.'

According to the report the tram stock was now down to 913 cars running over 102 route miles. Thus the RT bus was going to be triumphant. LT had nailed its colours to the mast, and as soon as sufficient diesel

buses became available, the trams would be scrapped. All the postwar talk was of new highways and an attempt to promote a balance between private motoring and the needs of public transport. Trams became an embarrassing anachronism; the clarion call of modernism was taken up by a number of writers. Harry Williams in his 1949 book, *South London*, extolls the virtues of the County of London Plan, where the past would be swept away – a past characterised by 'The traffic, obsolescent or antiquated in many cases – notably the trams and the high proportion of horse-drawn vehicles – which has reached a peak of confusion.' Williams was nothing if not poetic in his next diatribe; he talks of South London as 'poor little shops standing cheek by jowl with poor little shops, and miles upon miles of silver-ribboned tramlines heralding the passing of rocking juggernauts along miles and miles of ill-lighted, monotonous thoroughfares . . .'

In fairness there was another side to South London and many people actually found 'silver-ribboned tramlines' attractive! Obviously, Williams did not appreciate the charm of conduit tracks in a road lined by plane trees, where the calm of a summer's day was broken by a newly painted red and cream tramcar swaying gently on its way. Nor was he of a mind to eulogise the ride from Eltham to Woolwich on the top deck of a route 44 or 46 car, where the architectural delights of the Progress Estate would give

way to the fields and tall elm trees of Woolwich Common. The final surprise being the stately elegance of the Royal Military Academy, before the tram descended into the hustle and bustle of the market in Beresford Square.

There were of course tramway enthusiasts who regularly bombarded local newspapers and the powers that be with letters condemning the waste of resources in dismantling the system. They suggested money could be put to better use in relocating the track, buying new rolling stock and investing in passenger loading islands. However, supporters and detractors alike could not ignore the expense involved in maintaining the conduit system. This method of current collection was effectively antiquated by the 1920s, but it spared many areas of London the alleged 'unsightliness' of overhead wires. By the 1940s it was on its last legs and its maintenance was a major task involving a work force of skilled permanent way staff, which in 1948 numbered around 800 men. This force was sorely tested in the bitter winter of 1947, when freezing temperatures, power cuts, outdated equipment and lack of investment all combined to produce a miserable time for the travelling public and the tramways department in particular. Ice-bound tracks were cleared by an elderly fleet of four wheel snow brooms, and many staff worked overtime towing stranded trams back to their respective depots. The fact that

Above left Car 382 was fitted with trolley skids in place of the conventional trolley wheel. This form of current collector was in common use on the trolleybuses, but its extension to trams was limited by this small experiment. Trolley skids fitted with a carbon insert were quieter and did not convey so much overhead noise through the pole to the car roof . The ex-Croydon vehicle is depicted in Newington Butts, just south of the Elephant and Castle junction. D.A.Thompson

Above Car 1912 is about to reverse somewhere near the imaginary boundary between Woolwich and Plumstead. To the left is the high wall surrounding the Royal Arsenal, and to the right is a new RTL type bus working route 122. The 122 was unusual in that diesel buses actually terminated on the forecourt of Bexleyheath Trolleybus Depot. R.Hubble

a significant proportion of London's trolley-bus and bus network suffered disruption did not seem to affect the judgement of those resident at 55 Broadway, who seemed quite happy to disregard the safety merits of rail-bound transport in getting people to their destinations in freezing weather and during the frequent and paralysing smogs which afflicted the capital. Although the network was not short of vehicles, the rolling stock situation was giving cause for concern. In an article entitled *Pattern for Road Services – 1947*, G. E Sinclair, Deputy General Manager (Road Services), made a brief statement:

'Trams have the biggest proportion of old stock, nearly 400 of the cars, more than two out of every five, being over twenty-five

Above The tram versus trolleybus debate in the 1930s was effectively won by the latter, and the triumph of the trackless would have been total but for the Second World War. On McLeod Road, Abbey Wood, the two forms of electric traction happily coexisted. The 698 trolleybus from Bexleyheath to Woolwich was introduced on 10th November 1935. It replaced former Erith tram route 98 and overlapped tram routes 36/38 as far as Woolwich Ferry. R.Hubble

Below Bridgefoot, Vauxhall is the setting for Car 1250 as it turns short of Victoria terminus and reverses on a crossover to return to Grove Park. The line of traffic and the Esso filling station are rather ominous signs for the future. The increase in motor car ownership from the late 1940s onwards resulted in more congestion on London's roads, a factor which was at least partly responsible for a number of tramway accidents and injuries to passengers boarding or alighting from tramcars. J.H.Meredith

years old, and the highest tribute has to be paid to those who operate and keep these vehicles in service . . . The decision is to replace tramcars with buses; to the reconstruction problems associated with this conversion much thought has been given, but all the foreseeable difficulties in obtaining supplies do not make the prospects of an early start very promising.'

Active work at London Transport was still preparing the ground for conversion to buses, and a large part of the effort centred on rebuilding tram depots to accept diesel buses. This, as it turned out, would cause some headaches before construction materials were made available. Much of the metropolitan infrastructure – roads, housing and utilities – had been damaged by the recent bombing and these projects had to take priority. Although new buses were filtering through from AEC and Leyland Motors, the trams were 'a long time a-dying' and this impression was enhanced at a press conference on 5th December 1947, when Lord Latham, the prospective Chairman of the new London Transport Executive, ignored the topic of tram replacement. This attitude was in line with a recent Government White Paper which announced the postponement of tram scrapping until such time as replacement buses were available.

Lord Latham had more to say on 12th January 1948. In a speech to the press he explained:

'We have a three stage bus plan for London: (1) to replace outworn buses, (2) to strengthen existing services, and (3) to open up new routes. The conversion of the South London tramcars will have to wait possibly five years because of the slowing down of manufacture of new buses due to national requirements. We spent £1,000,000 on the tramways in 1947 to keep them in the highest state of efficiency pending replacement.'

An interesting foreign view of LT's plans can be gleaned from an article written in the Hanover Tramways staff magazine by Herr Scharnhorst. He comments on an official visit he paid to London Transport:

'Since 1932 no new tramway extensions have been opened. It is freely admitted that the 37 routes in use today are especially well suited for special events and peak hour traffic. Despite this, they have not been modernised; it is intended instead to replace the trams with about 1,000 buses, commencing 1st October 1950. This despite the fact that the trams carried 292 million passengers in 1949 with 52.8 million car kilometres.' The citizens of Hanover were to benefit enormously from an upgraded and modernised tramway system, so there must have been some relief that Herr Scharnhorst was not influenced by LT policy.

Meanwhile throughout 1948 track repairs were continuing and these included (at long last) new loading islands at Streatham Hill and South Lambeth Road. Early in the year permanent way work was noted along Kennington Road, Clapham High Street, Clapham Road and parts of the Victoria Embankment. It was further announced that the year's programme would include the repair of some 15 miles of track, and this would eventually cover locations such as Vauxhall Roundabout, Brixton Road, Camberwell New Road, Lavender Hill, Borough Road and Upper Tooting Road. Official sources stated that deliveries of steel rail would exceed 2,000 tons for the year. It must be remembered that motormen in London used magnetic track brakes for normal service stops. Although soft iron was used for the brake shoes, there must have been additional track wear. One example that comes to mind was by Tylecroft Road, Norbury, where the section of track where brakes were applied was renewed in the post-war period.

On the vehicle side many cars were repainted and indicator blinds were cleaned and replaced. Ex-Croydon cars 378-380, 382, 387 and 398 were fitted with trolley skids rather than the more conventional trolley wheel. It would seem that the intention may have been to confine these vehicles to route 42, but in the event they also took turns on trunk routes 16/18. At the same time several Feltham type cars had quick release valves fitted to their air brake equipment, recog-

nisable by a sharp 'hiss' when released. The staff at Charlton Works managed to effect repairs on over 420 trams during 1948.

Some idea of the genuine affection tram staff had for their department can be gleaned from an article in the April 1948 issue of *London Transport Magazine*. It records a mammoth effort from 60 motorman, conductors and permanent way staff who volunteered to clean out the Kingsway Subway in the early hours of Good Friday. Shortage of labour was blamed for the fact that this task had been neglected. The volunteer force consisted of employees from Holloway and Camberwell depots, and the job was completed in time for the first tram at six o'clock on Good Friday morning.

Above Former Walthamstow Car 2053 makes an exit from the Vauxhall gyratory traffic system. The track in these parts was heavily used and at peak times was traversed by around 270 trams per hour. This 54 heads into Harleyford Road on 22nd September 1951. Car 205 may not be going at top speed, but it is probably demonstrating that other characteristic of ex-Walthamstow cars – their unique and penetrating gear and truck noise – which made this type sound, according to one enthusiast, "like a barrel of nuts and bolts revolving in an air raid siren!" J.H.Meredith

Below Ice and snow could play havoc on the roads, but the trams being railbound at least stood a chance of battling their way through. In this endeavour they were helped by the fleet of snow brooms such as 037 which is sweeping the tracks in Islington. The motorman of Car 2002, southbound to West Norwood via the Kingsway Subway, passes without a sideways glance. He probably takes for granted he has a good support team.

In this picture it is deceptively quiet, bearing in mind this was the main road leading to Blackwall. Tunnel. The family getting off Car 1885 seemed to have all the time in the world to reach the pavement. It is likely they lived in one of the nearby "prefabs" which were constructed along Tunnel Avenue and Blackwall Lane. At the end of the twentieth century, the gas holder behind the tram gave way to another imposing structure – the Greenwich Dome.

On 7th September, cars stored out of service in Purley Depot, many of which had originally come from Hampstead Depot, were shifted to accommodation at Wandsworth Depot. It had been decided to use Purley as a repair facility to help out the hard pressed staff at the CRD.

A brief mention should be made of major service alterations in the immediate post-war era – details of routes can be found in the Appendix – alterations before 1949 can be summarised as follows:

On 19th June 1946, all-night routes were allocated numbers, and on 29th October 1947, Kingsway Subway route 31 was extended weekdays to terminate at Islington Green (Agricultural Hall on indicator blinds). On 3rd January 1948, improvements were made to Saturday services on routes 24, 34 and 74. Route extensions along existing track included on 5th May 1948, the prolonging of route 44 from its historic terminus outside St John's Church in Eltham to a crossover opposite the Yorkshire Grey at Eltham Green. This spot was known in the tramway department as Middle Park Avenue, and this reflected the temperance tradition of the LCC whereby local hostelries never appeared on indicator blinds! In June, route 40 cars were extended eastwards from Parry Street to a terminate at a crossover opposite Perrott Street, Woolwich. However, at peak hours, cars still worked as far as Wickham Lane, Plumstead.

Atmospheric pollution hit the headlines late in the year when a blanket of smog enveloped the capital. This particular 'pea souper' was not all bad news. On 5th December 1948, an LT official departed somewhat

Another route extension which made sense was the working of the 74s right through to Grove Park terminus. Car 1007 looks particularly smart in this picture taken outside Lewisham Town Hall in Catford. The date is 10th July 1949. J.H.Meredith

from the 'party line' to admit on air in the BBC Light Programme:

'In the morning no trolleybus could leave the depot. It was the same all over North London. Things were much better in South London. We still have the trams there!' It should be remembered that, at this time, most London houses were heated with coal fires, and that coal was rationed and of poor quality, therefore in calm winter weather the mist became a thick, yellow fog. Trams normally kept running in these conditions, albeit very slowly. The worst problem for the crew was putting the trolley on the wire at change pits and suburban termini. Street lighting of this era was in many respects antiquated and the Metropolitan Borough of Wandsworth, for example, still relied on gas lamps to illuminate important thoroughfares. One tramway enthusiast who went successfully from Norbury to the Embankment and back several times in smog conditions, noted that on one journey the tram passed a line of abandoned buses up Brixton Hill, extending for about half a mile.

Thus 1948 bowed out. It was very much a 'make do and mend' time for the tramways, and those who lobbied on behalf of the rail bound vehicles could be heartened by the fact that their replacement did not appear imminent. However, as we shall see, the gloom was to deepen when it was revealed that the trams had lost just over one million pounds in the year. The following twelve months finally put paid to any false hopes, and preparations for the demise of the London tramcar gathered momentum in 1949.

Above This is the interior of Car 295, a tram which started life in the West Ham fleet. The couple on the end bench seat have a better than usual view of the motorman as he has omitted to close the bulkhead door. Although this practice was officially frowned upon, in summer on hot, airless days it was often the case that the door was kept open to encourage a pleasant breeze through the lower saloon. It is the last day of operation, which could account for the fact that the fare chart on the left bulkhead has already disappeared into someone's collection! A.B.Cross

Facing page Car 99 was from the former East Ham fleet. It is stationed outside the queuing pens by the Royal Arsenal Gate. Note the way the trolley rope is fed through a pigtail (the corkscrew attachment on the top deck) and is fastened on the dash next to the fleet number. Automatic trolley retrievers, common in North America, were never popular in the UK. On the right hand side of the tram underneath the driver's mirror is the blue and white 39 running number. Other features of note are the fog lamp positioned just to the left of the indicator box and the T shaped metal insert to keep the vestibule from disintegrating. A.B.Cross

TRAMCARS

THE AVERAGE Londoner out for a stroll along the Victoria Embankment might have assumed all trams looked alike. On closer inspection he might have noticed the distinctive design of the Felthams with their projecting cabs, but otherwise the rest of the vehicles passing him by were much of a muchness – large red and cream double deckers with eight wheels and a conduit plough underneath and on top a trolley pole. Of course, to a tramway worker this opinion was a gross oversimplification. Each class of tram presented different characteristics; to the motorman some cars were tricky to han-

dle, some were underpowered, some difficult to brake; to the passenger, trams could be noisy, uncomfortable and draughty, whilst the Felthams were pleasant and inviting; to the mechanical staff at Charlton Works some cars were easy to maintain and others were a dead loss! Regular passengers might swear that a particular tram had a personality all of its own. As with all well-loved machines each tram was referred to as 'she', sometimes with a tone of resignation, when a motorman would yell out to his conductor, 'the old gal is playing up this morning!' as he wrestled with a defective controller or jammed brakes.

Official figures issued in 1945 listed the fleet strength at 1,006 cars; of these about 100 were stored at Hampstead Depot. This building in Cressy Road had been maintained throughout the war as an emergency

depository for crash victims, trams displaced by trolleybus conversions, trams awaiting windscreens and trams awaiting scrapping. It occasionally hosted visiting delegations from provincial cities who were seeking extra vehicles to help out with the war effort. A party from Sheffield almost decided to relieve London Transport of some of its ex-West Ham and ex-East Ham trams, made redundant by the June 1940 conversion of the Commercial Road trunk routes, but caution prevailed and the Steel City decided to stick with four wheel cars acquired cheaply from Bradford and Newcastle.

Access to Hampstead Depot, after the local routes had been converted to trolley-buses in July 1938, was maintained by a lengthy single track connection from Holloway Depot via Kentish Town, Prince of Wales Road, Malden Road and Agincourt Road. During March 1947 Hampstead Depot was vacated by most trams. Cars were driven to Purley Depot where they rejoined some others of the 'reserve fleet'.

At the end of 1947 the stock had shrunk to 871 trams. The pace of disposals then slackened, and by the end of 1948 there were some 530 'standards', E/1 type cars from the former London County Council fleet. Amongst these were 93 trams, built to a very similar design to the LCC E/1, which had been acquired from the former Croydon, East Ham, Walthamstow and West Ham systems. The 'modern' fleet consisted of LCC classes E/3 and HR/2, and of course type UCC, the Felthams.

The ex-London County Council E/1s represented the backbone of the fleet. They were delivered from Scottish car builder Hurst Nelson, in batches from May 1907 to October 1909; they bore the fleet numbers 752–1426. Brush of Loughborough, secured the contract to supply a further 200 cars. These were numbered 1477–1676 and the final tram was delivered in 1911. After the war, Hurst Nelson and Brush split a further order, and in 1922, cars 1727–1851 completed the series – these trams were always associated with Clapham Depot. The bodywork of the standard E/1 was basically wood with metal dashes and staircases, and each car rode on two maximum traction trucks. This type of truck consisted of two wheels, known as the 'drivers', which were larger that the two 'pony' wheels which made up the rest of the truck or bogie. The two sets of pony wheels faced the plough carrier which was situated midway under the tram. All vehicles were equipped with a plough carrier for the conduit system, and most had two trolley poles, one for each direction, for the overhead sections. The rehab cars of 1935–37 have already been mentioned, suffice to say that some of these reconditioned

Above This line of 'standards' in New Cross Road is headed by Car 1409 which retains the Venner route stencil in the front top deck window. This vehicle dates from 1909–10, has two Westinghouse controllers operating two 42hp Westinghouse 220 type motors. It weighs a total of 16.3 tons (16.5 tonnes). The tram behind is Car 579, a member of the 1930 group of E/ls. It also has Westinghouse electrical equipment, but differs outwardly from a standard E/1 by virtue of its double width centre pillars in the lower saloon and the larger E/3 type route number box on the top deck.

Below The conductor of Car 1663 and his lady passenger look as if they've both lost a shilling and found sixpence! Aside from the glum expressions, we can observe the mixed nature of the lower deck seating. The original moquette on some seats has been replaced by a rexine material, normally reserved for the upper deck, where the smokers would congregate. The right hand bulkhead window was tinted a dull orange colour to prevent glare from the lower saloon reflecting on the driver's windscreen at night.

E/1s possessed only one trolley pole, and these vehicles were despatched to Penhall Road Scrapyard before many of their older, unrebuilt sisters.

The fitting of driver's windscreens in the 1930s had obviously enhanced the appearance of these trams, as well as improved the protection offered to the motorman and conductor. However, the general impression given by this class of tram in the post-war years was one of obsolescence. Indeed, some cars still had 46 wooden backed seats on the top deck. Passenger comfort in the lower (non-smoking) saloon was reasonable; there were 27 upholstered seats. On both decks, all transverse seats were reversible, and at each terminus it was the task of the conductor to flip the seatbacks over, so that passengers faced the direction of travel. Although the E/1s were an improvement on earlier open top models, travellers in winter still had to face the prospect of no heating inside the tram. This could make journeys, especially in the upper saloon, very cold indeed. The state of some trams in the post-war era was, quite frankly, lamentable; an example of this run-down state of affairs was Car 1420 which was described by one observer, Father Benedict Sankey, thus:

More than once towards the end of the war, or just after it, I had noticed 1420 – generally at Victoria. This must have been one of the trams brought back into service as result of the war; it had wartime vestibules with those horrid 'canvas bandages' between the woodwork and the original low dashes at either end. Nothing rare about that, but 1420 was particularly dirty, faded and generally unkempt. Its paintwork was the darkest red I've ever seen, and there was rust on the upper deck panelling. No doubt it was a New Cross car, and though a good many trams were rundown and scruffy, this one was exceptional.

It should be noted that New Cross Depot was the largest on the system, and it was also well known for its less-than-perfect standard of maintenance. Not only were some cars poorly maintained, but many of the oldest vehicles were 'working loose' and consequently, they received metal bracing

Above left A close up of an E/1 truck reveals details of the axle boxes and the magnetic brake shoe. On the extreme left can be glimpsed one set of channel irons belonging to the plough carrier. D.A.Thompson

Above The interior top deck of Car 1291 reflects a rather spartan state of affairs with wooden seats, wooden slats on the floor and matchboarded panelling. A bulkhead door gives access to one staircase and the mirror was used by the crew to check on passengers in the upper saloon. The date is 27th July 1950. A.B.Cross

Below The 1777–1851 series was always associated with Clapham Depot. Cars 1798 and 1819 are seen on home territory. Both have Brush bodies, Hurst Nelson trucks, English Electric controllers and two 63hp EE motors. The leading vehicle also sports metal straps which serve as body bracing. Note the three discs above the indicator box, these were employed as coloured lenses before the introduction in 1912 of route numbers. Thus cars working after dark from Clapham to Southwark Bridge would have shown red-white-green to aid potential passengers. J.H.Meredith

straps to keep the lower saloon from disintegrating further. Front vestibules could also develop leaks, and it was not unusual to see a sandbag employed to plug the hole. Charlton Works did try to keep up with the task of maintaining the fleet and official British Transport Commission statistics issued for the period 22nd May to 18th June 1950 listed the following numbers of trams being worked on:

Heavy repairs carried out	18
Light repairs carried out	49
Total operating stock	830
Trams awaiting repair in workshops	30
Trams awaiting repair in depots ...	87
Available operating stock	713
Available operating stock at same date in 1949	731

Fleet numbers 552–601 were allocated to the 1930 delivery of E/1 trams. These cars used electrical equipment from single deck class F and G trams withdrawn when the Kingsway Subway was rebuilt to accommodate double deckers. This batch could always be recognised by the wide pillar separating the central windows in the lower saloon. They gained a reputation for being underpowered and many were allocated by New Cross Depot to the 'slow road', which was the nickname for docklands routes 68 and 70.

Cars 81–100 were inherited from the former East Ham Corporation fleet. They were similar in appearance to the standards, and dated from the mid-1920s. They acquitted themselves well in terms of mechanical performance and had the edge over their fellow East Londoners from West Ham, which were generally slower. Ex-West Ham cars carried fleet numbers in the 295–344 series, and could always be recognised by the route number box beneath the top deck front window, a feature they also shared with rehab cars. Another peculiarity was their narrow spaced advert mouldings, which mercifully prevented all this class from being plastered with the dreaded LAST TRAM WEEK posters.

The last refugees from East London were the ex-Walthamstow cars in the 2042–2061 series. These solidly built vehicles were characterised by rather heavy looking windscreen vestibules. On the mechanical side they were noisy but fast, in fact they were known to enthusiasts as 'rockets', and not only could they outpace the rest of the tram fleet, but they could also show a clean pair of heels to most members of LT's Central Bus Department. At least two trams of this group were partly rehabilitated inside, the seating and decor in both saloons approaching that of a reconditioned E/1. On the debit side, they were rough riding, and it was said that the corner seats on the ex-Walthamstows

Above Trams in the 552–601 series were distinctive in having wide centre pillars. They were also badly underpowered, a fact which did not seem to harm their survival chances, as many went right on to the end of the line on 5th July 1952. Car 577 is pictured at Eltham Green roundabout whilst working route 44. Under the front stairs the motorman seems to have borrowed the tool kit belonging to Car 1859.

Below The ex-Walthamstow cars were the eccentrics of the post-war fleet. Fast, furious and very noisy, an approaching Walthamstow was the enfant terrible of many a South London high street. Their appearance was not helped by heavy, chunky looking vestibules as demonstrated by Car 2052 in Brighton Road, South Croydon. The motorman of this tram will very shortly have to shut off power as he coasts under the section feed in the overhead wires. If he forgets this simple rule, the motorist at the corner of Bartlett Street will be able to witness a firework display of electrical arcing from the trolley wheel of the passing tram.

were always in a depressed condition where passengers had been bounced up and down so much!

The final members of the E/1 family were the 23 trams contributed by Croydon Corporation. They dated from 1926 and took numbers in the series 375–399. A distinguishing feature of the ex-Croydon vehicles was the oval, rugby ball shaped hole at the side of the plough carrier.

Last but not least were cars 2, 982, 1103, 1260, 1370 and 1444. The last two formed their own sub-class (ME/3), having been rebuilt from single truck M class cars. All six trams were outwardly very similar, with reconditioned top decks featuring angled window pillars which gave a semi-stream-lined effect.

Above Only four ex-Croydon trams got the rehab treatment (cars 376, 379, 380 and 398). Here is the last of the batch in High Street, Thornton Heath, at the corner of Grange Road. All Croydon vehicles could be instantly recognised by the oval hole in the side of the plough carrier. Car 398 was reconditioned in November 1936 and decommissioned in January 1952. B.T.Cooke

Below Car 1444 was also from the small and exclusive ME/3 stable. It is pictured on 25th July 1948 at Eltham Green roundabout. It was first reconditioned in May 1932, but it was later damaged in an accident and rebuilt with a domed roof in October 1934. It was withdrawn in May 1951. B.T.Cooke

Below left A closer look at Car 1444 reveals the handbrake shoes, sand pipe to the rails, front step and the rear of the lifeguard tray.

Above The trucks of E/3 Car 1918 are clearly shown in this view of the entrance to Telford Avenue Depot. Note especially the chain to each bogie which restricted excessive lateral movement, and the magnetic brakes suspended between the driving and pony wheels of each truck. B.T.Cooke

Left This study of the platform of Car 187 shows the relative positions of the controller, staircase and handrails. Just visible at the foot of the stairs is the gong pedal which produced an audible warning for other road users. Note that the motorman had to stand at his job, although on this fine summer's day with all the windows open, it probably wasn't such a hardship. D.A.Thompson

Facing page

Above To all intents and purposes Car 1938 was a regular member of class E/3 working service 18 near Streatham Hill Station on 26th March 1951. However, on this occasion someone has forgotten to remove the via Kingsway Subway glass from the indicator box. The tram also shows off a newly cut 18 route stencil; some of these were later 'recycled' by some judicious hacksaw work into 48 stencils! Note the Metropolitan Stage Carriage Licence No. 9036 on the lower bulkhead. One of these was displayed at one end of every London tram. J.H.Meredith

Below left Car 160 was a 'one off', the only trolleyless E/3. It seated 28 in the lower saloon and 46 in the upper, and it had two 57.5hp motors and English Electric controllers. It went for scrap in April 1952. D.Battams

Below right HR/2 Car 120 had high backed seats on the lower deck which were allegedly the bane of conductors at termini like Victoria where a quick turnaround was vital. This picture was taken on 10th November 1947 at the Embankment where services 56/84 looped, therefore sparing the conductor all the rushing about. At the other end by Peckham Rye, he would have more time to rearrange the seating. G.F.Ashwell

The 'modern' element of the fleet consisted of cars belonging to classes E/3, HR/2 and UCC. First and foremost was the candidate for London's most famous tram, the former LCC 'Bluebird', Car 1. This tram was conceived as a prototype of a further 100 cars, but the advent of the LPTB put paid to any purchase of new rolling stock. Car 1 was unique; it had comfortable seating and straight staircases connected upper and lower saloons. Separate driving cabs were provided for the motorman, who also had air brakes at his disposal. Telford Avenue Depot was the homebase for this vehicle, and it was often active on peak hour services from Streatham to the Embankment.

The other ex-LCC cars, dating from 1930–31, were of more conventional design than Car 1. Classes E/3 and HR/2 had identical bodywork, but the former rode on two motor, maximum traction trucks, whilst the latter class was equipped with four motor, equal wheel trucks. As might be inferred from this information, the more powerful HR/2 cars were ordered specifically with hilly routes in mind, particularly those services which climbed Dog Kennel Hill, Dulwich and Highgate Hill (Highgate Hill route 11 was converted to trolleybuses in December 1939). The E/3s were designated to work the Kingsway Subway routes 31, 33 and 35. Wooden bodied cars were not usually permitted to run through the Subway, due to the risk of fire; therefore, the all-metal bodied E/3s were eminently suited for this task. The only 'fly in the ointment' with the HR/2 class cars was that the batch numbered 101–159 did not possess trolley poles. Thus, they were restricted to conduit routes, and lacked the versatility of their sister vehicles. The other HR/2 trams were numbered in the series 1854–1897, and the E/3s were 1904–2003. Fleet numbers 161–210 were reserved for E/3 cars supplied to Leyton and these had Alpax metal framed driver's windscreens right from the start. Car 160 was officially designated as a member of class E/3, but it did not have trolley gear. LCC cars were subsequently fitted with rather handsome Alpax windscreens. Unfortunately, towards the end of the tramway era, many of these had been replaced by austerity looking wooden screens, and this detracted from their appearance. In fact it was quite common to see a tram with non-matching vestibules – Alpax one end, and wooden at the other. These vehicles could always be recognised, because on the remaining Alpax screen, the black lining on the window pillars was omitted.

Not everything that happened to these trams was of an austerity nature. It was noted by *Modern Tramway* in June 1951, that several of classes HR/2 and E/3 had

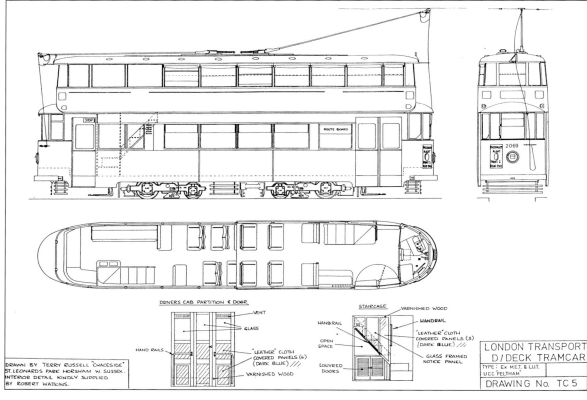

been recently renovated. Cars 120 and 210 were singled out for praise, and the former of these, with its rotating seats in the lower saloon, was considered by *Modern Tramway* to be the best car in the fleet.

Type UCC or Feltham trams were the most striking trams owned by London Transport. Their modern design incorporated comfortable seating, straight staircases, a bulkhead-free top deck, air brakes and separate driver's cabs. In post-war years the front exits fell into disuse and they were normally only employed by motormen as a short cut to the driver's cab. They could be speedy cars, but rather let themselves down when it came to tackling gradients. Trucks were equipped with roller bearings, and these produced a very free running car which could easily coast along roads which were level or had a slight downgrade. The Felthams were slightly wider than standard cars and this enabled transverse double seats to be installed in the lower saloon. Although the seating capacity, at 66, was lower than the 73 accommodated on a standard E/1, the lower deck vestibules could each hold 10 standing passengers, and this extra capacity was much appreciated in peak hours.

The air brakes were not automatic, and some motormen always seemed to experience difficulties with this non-standard

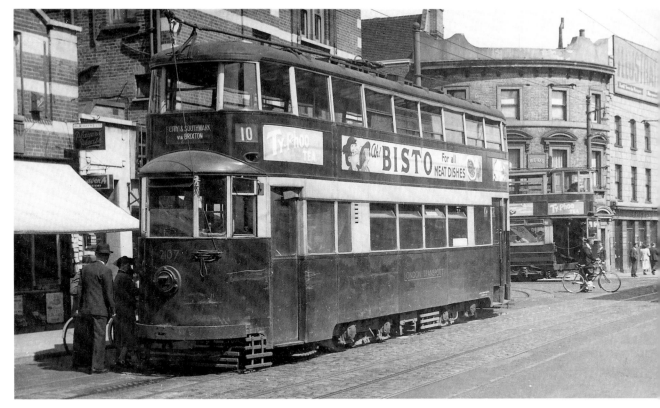

Right Feltham Car 2107 was originally built for the Metropolitan Electric Tramways in 1930–31 as Car 363. By the time this photo was taken the front exits had become disused and passengers boarded and alighted in the traditional fashion at the rear. This vehicle was withdrawn in January 1951 and dispatched to Leeds where it received the fleet number 541.

Below right Car 2167 was the last experimental Feltham to survive. It is depicted here at Thornton Heath Pond. As can be observed, it had lower cabs than the production Felthams, and had an attractive expanse of cream paint to offset the LT red. It was originally numbered MET Car 330 and was scrapped in December 1949.

equipment. In fact many Felthams typically stopped with a shudder of slack brake rigging. As mentioned in the previous chapter, the make do and mend philosophy was sometimes quite apparent, and one car was noted in 1948 with five different patterns of moquette on the seats in the lower saloon! However, in many respects, this class was probably one of the finest ever to grace the London streets. Most passengers still recall the light and airy interiors, and the feeling of comfortable spaciousness which these vehicles conveyed. They were also fitted with heaters, a feature almost unknown in most British public transport vehicles of that era.

Feltham trams inherited from the London United Tramways received numbers 2120–2164, and those which came from the Metropolitan Electric Tramways were numbered in the 2066–2119 series. Only one former experimental Feltham survived and this was Car 2167. The Felthams were based at Telford Avenue Depot, which had a record for poor maintenance of the trams in its charge. They also strayed into Brixton Hill Depot, which was effectively an annex of Telford Avenue. Unfortunately, this class of car was restricted to routes 8, 10, 16, 18, 20, 22 and 24, although they were permitted to visit Charlton Works on non-passenger visits.

Above left Works car 011 dated from 1909 and its chief function was to transport wheels, axles and motors between Charlton Works (seen here) and other depots. The axles were permitted a certain amount of lateral movement to adjust to the curvature of the track. There is almost no protection for the crew and driving this thing on a rainy day must have been a thoroughly damp experience! LCCTT

Above right Car 03 was originally ordered by the LCC in 1905. It carried a large capacity water tank which connected to rail grinding equipment. Carburundum blocks were fitted to smooth off rail corrugations. This phenomenon caused the sound of 'roaring rails' and it was a particular nuisance inside the Kingsway Subway.

Car 2 was reconditioned in February 1935 and had Metrovick motors and controllers. It was constructed using the frame and trucks of the original Car 1370, and it also sported a domed roof surmounting inward tapering window frames. It survived until the last day of the system. D.A.Thompson

The works car fleet was rather a motley collection of four wheelers, some of which had been converted from former passenger cars. Rail grinders 02, 04 and 014 were joined by stores vans 05, 06, 08, 09, 010 and 015, plus the distinctive open, wheel carrier vans 011 and 012. Snowbrooms 016–026, 028, 029, 031–037 were former class B and C vehicles which had been modified for their new duties. They were often seen on active duty during the winter months, and were sometimes called upon to work round the clock to keep tracks clear of snow and ice.

All London Transport tramcars in the 1949–52 era were turned out in the standard LT red and cream livery. Where the two colours were adjacent a black line was placed between them. Other ornamentation was minimal; each dash was lined out in yellow, and the fleet numerals together with the

London Transport name on the side of the car were in gold with thin black edging. Fenders, trucks, conduit carriers, undergear and controllers were painted black. Roofs on some trams were brown oxide, but latterly a standard dark grey was used. The interior colour scheme featured white for ceilings and window pillars, and dark brown from the window sills to the floor. Some cars had brighter interiors, with blue replacing the dark brown.

As previously mentioned, certain cars had very individual characteristics, for instance, Car 960 was forever going wrong. Eventually, the fault was traced to the wiring and remedied by the staff at the CRD. Other trams that stood out from the rest were E/3s 1938 and 1941 which were used on the late night 33 staff car which ran Norwood – Oval – Camberwell Green – Milkwood Road –

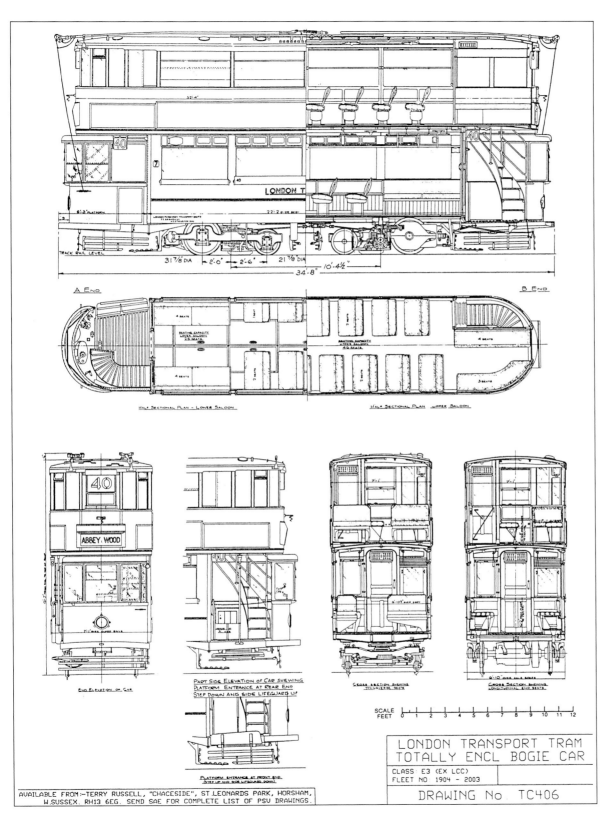

A END

B END

Half Sectional Plan - Lower Saloon

Half Sectional Plan - Upper Saloon

40

ABBEY WOOD

End Elevation of Car

Part Side Elevation of Car Shewing
Platform Entrance at Rear End
Step Down and Side Lifeguard Up

Platform Entrance at Front End.
(Step Up and Side Lifeguard Down)

Cross Section Shewing
Transverse Seats

Cross Section Shewing
Longitudinal End Seats

SCALE
FEET 0 1 2 3 4 5 6 7 8 9 10 11 12

LONDON TRANSPORT TRAM
TOTALLY ENCL BOGIE CAR

CLASS E3 (EX LCC)
FLEET NO 1904 - 2003

DRAWING No. TC406

AVAILABLE FROM:- TERRY RUSSELL, "CHACESIDE", ST.LEONARDS PARK, HORSHAM, W.SUSSEX. RH13 6EG. SEND SAE FOR COMPLETE LIST OF PSU DRAWINGS.

Class E/3, fleet numbers
1904–2003. Terry Russell

Norwood. These particular vehicles were considered amongst the quietest in the fleet. Another E/3, Car 1991, had an extra series notch on the controller which gave it a higher top speed. Car 1989 was unpopular with crews due to its bucket seats on the lower deck. These were a particular nuisance at Victoria terminus in peak hours, where passengers alighted from one end of the tram at the same time as people boarded the other end . . . The conductor would have great difficulty in turning all the seats and coping with the flow of passengers.

The ex-Croydon fleet was also a mixed bunch. Car 391 was very sound mechanically and the internal seating had been recovered in brown rexine, giving the passenger accom-

modation a very smart appearance. On the other hand, Car 399 was the black sheep of the Croydon family. The bodywork was so shot to pieces that the movement between the upper and lower saloons was clearly visible. The top deck bench seats next to the stairwell were secured to the roof of the lower saloon, but the panelling of the upper saloon bulkhead seemed to sway independently of the tram, with the result that passengers on these seats received a sharp blow in the back every time Car 399 bucked and pitched at speed. Cars 390 and 393 were also to be avoided as their upholstered top deck seats had been replaced by wooden ones from scrapped E/1s.

Feltham Car 2165 was turned out in

splendid state, but was dismally under-powered; it had received trucks from experimental Car 2317 'Poppy', scrapped in 1935. A trip up Brixton Hill on Car 2165 was a painfully slow affair.

On standard, unreconditioned cars destination indicator boxes were affixed at each end of the tram. Usually two lines of destination information could be displayed; the lettering was white on a black background. E/1 cars from the 552–601 series, E/3s and HR/2s were originally equipped with K-Ray destination boxes. These had three lamps above the roller blind, rather than behind it, and it was claimed this arrangement made the lettering more visible at night. Cars working services 31, 33 and 35 possessed a coloured top slide (white letters on a blue background) on their K-Ray boxes which read VIA KINGSWAY SUBWAY. Many HR/2 cars had blue bulbs illuminating the destination blinds. On reconditioned cars the recessed indicator displays had room for a three line display, but in practice many cars had the top of the glass painted out, which only left room for the standard two line display.

Route number stencils varied in size. The largest could be found on E/3, HR/2, E/1 series 552–601, ex-Croydon and ex-Walthamstow cars. Each large stencil measured 22½in (570mm) by 15½in (673mm). Some E/1s still had their Venner stencils which dated from 1913. These were 26½in (673mm) long and 8½in (216mm) deep. Smaller side stencils were sometimes carried in the right bottom corner of the lower saloon window nearest the platform; these measured 11in (280mm) by 10in (254mm).

Less obvious to the general public was the small blue and white number allocated to each tram, which showed the position of the tram as regards other trams working the same service. These were originally known by LCC employees as route numbers (pronounced 'rowt'), but were also referred to as running numbers. Extra trams drafted in for peak hour working received running numbers upwards from the highest number shown by regular service cars. The extra trams were known as 'swingers'. Unlike LT buses and trolleybuses, trams never displayed a depot code; on the side of each conductor's ticket box, however, a duty number indicated to which depot he belonged.

Route boards, or 'slip' boards, were carried in brackets fixed just under the two central windows on the bottom deck. These had a pale cream or off-white background

The four tracks on Dog Kennel Hill earned a place in tramway mythology. Only four-motor HR/2 class cars were permitted to work the gradient. Car 1869 descends in a controlled manner. R.Hubble

with black lettering. The boards could be reversed, and on the back they carried the message CHEAP MIDDAY FARES in white on a red background. Below the end two windows of the lower saloon, two smaller slip boards gave information on intermediate locations. These featured white lettering on a blue background. A typical example was shown on route 40 trams where one board would state TO & FROM GREENWICH PIER AND BEACH for those making a day trip or a summer Sunday excursion, whilst the other targeted sports' fans with NEAR CHARLTON FOOTBALL GROUND.

Advertising had been used extensively by both municipal and company tramways, and this tradition was carried on by London

In its latter days Car 1 wandered around like a lost soul. Only a few motormen were willing and able to handle it, and consequently it mostly ventured out only at peak hours. Here it is pictured outside the LCC Fire Brigade HQ on Albert Embankment.

Transport. Indeed, many of the adverts added a splash of colour to an otherwise drab looking car. For those firms thinking of promoting their wares in this fashion, a 'Wholeside' measuring 20ft (6.1m) by 20in (509mm) was on offer for £16 per annum. A 'Demi-side' measuring 12ft 6in (3.8m) by 21½in (546mm), of which there were two each side of the longer Feltham cars, was priced at £14 per annum.

Above Car 2138 glides across the intersection at the Elephant and Castle. In the background is the famous Guinness Clock, a well known local landmark which was illuminated at night. New Kent Road leads off to the right past the Trocadero. The planners had had their eyes on this junction for many years and an LCC plan of the late 1920s envisaged a large roundabout at this spot with the tram tracks altered accordingly. Since the trams were abandoned the whole area has undergone major reconstruction and now looks very different.

Below This may look like mayhem at the Elephant, but in theory all entrances to the junction were controlled by traffic lights. Car 1909 has just emerged from London Road and is southbound into Newington Butts and Kennington Park Road. Driving a tram across here took skill as there were several dead sections of conduit, and every tram driver had to anticipate the behaviour of other road users so that he did not have to stop at an inconvenient point. If the worst came to the worst, the marooned motorman would have to wait for a gentle push from a following tram to resume his journey. D.A. Thompson

THIS YEAR was a crucial one for the tramways. Any lingering hopes that the decision makers of the London Transport Executive were about to undertake a tram ride on the road to Damascus, were finally extinguished by a series of official announcements. The presence of the tramcar on London's streets was an embarrassment to the capital's postwar planners, and as such it was cited as an obstacle to all manner of traffic improvement schemes. Major reconstruction of several important bottlenecks such as the junction at the Elephant and Castle, was put on hold until tram tracks could be removed. Several local councils expressed the belief that traffic flows would speed up, thus enhancing the quality of life for their citizens. The new ring roads and their associated feeder sub arterial highways, as envisaged in the *County of London Plan*, promised a wholesale 'rejuvenation' of the metropolitan area. Tramways, modern or otherwise, did not enter the equation.

The year got off to the worst possible start with a tram workers' strike on Saturday 1st January. In those days it must be remembered that this was not a public holiday and normal services were run. However, not on this day! Crews from every depot withdrew their labour in an effort to convince management that they should receive extra pay for working after 1pm on Saturdays. The only exception to this mass walk out was at Thornton Heath where staff worked normally, but observed the 'operational niceties' of the situation by only operating routes 16/18 as far as the LCC boundary at Norbury – route 42 ran as usual. The whole matter eventually went to arbitration and duties on Saturday afternoons were settled on a time and a quarter basis. Tram and trolleybus crews received 8½ pence an hour more, and this prompted a Transport & General Workers Union official at New Cross Depot to remark that he would recommend the crews to accept the award – 'after all, half a loaf is better than none', he added in a tone of resignation.

Aside from personnel affairs, relations with local councils were often strained by the allegation that London Transport was neglecting its duties *vis-a-vis* the maintenance of the permanent way. Rails were on the agenda of Bermondsey Safety Committee when, on 14th January, they petitioned the LTE to supply more men to repair the tram tracks in the borough. Their message had some effect, because a subsequent inspection

by V. Field, the Borough Surveyor, accompanied by LT representatives, resulted in a mobile gang being sent to repair the ten worst points and crossings. Mr Field was quoted as saying that London Transport had great difficulty in getting suitable men to repair the tracks, because it was considered a dead end job, as trams would eventually be scrapped. More excavations were noted on 28th January, outside the site of the old Marius Road Depot in Balham High Road. A deep hole several feet in length had been dug below the southbound track. The conduit was disconnected, thus obliging trams to coast across the gap in power supply.

It was announced that 52-year-old J. R. Garwood, who started work as a tram conductor in 1919, had just been appointed Divisional Superintendent at the Vauxhall headquarters of LT Trams and Trolleybuses, Southern Area. One of his first official duties was to point out in the January Traffic Circular that bridge repairs at East Dulwich Station would temporarily reduce road widths. Tram drivers were warned to proceed dead slow at this point, and conductors were requested to stand on the rear platform and ensure that the chain was across, thus preventing any passenger from alighting.

The month ended with traders in Balham High Road complaining about all night trams and the noise they made. It was alleged that thieves waited for a passing tramcar to muffle the sound of breaking a shop window. LT's reply to the criticism was that they had instructed motormen 'to go as quietly as possible'. The Executive regretted they could not use buses instead, because 'there were no bus garages on the route.'

Left Cars from Thornton Heath Depot were the only ones operating on New Year's Day 1949. Car 383 waits at the narrow entrance for the right of way on to London Road. A part of the rather cramped car sheds can be glimpsed behind the emerging tram. Obviously this was unsuitable for bus operation and LT promptly published plans for demolition of several adjacent properties as well as the former Croydon Corporation offices and depot. G.E.Baddeley

Below The state of the permanent way concerned everyone. Wartime maintenance arrears and lack of materials in the late 1940s had hindered the effort to remedy the situation. This particular stretch is in Woolwich Road, Charlton. Note the 'dished' rail joints and the sunken, dislodged setts. C.Carter

Camberwell Green in this picture seems to be free of the queuing trams which were the bane of Mr Southernwood (as explained in the text below). Ex-Croydon rehab Car 380 crosses from Camberwell New Road on its eastwards journey to Woolwich, whilst in the opposite direction, one of the latest products from the Ford Motor Company leads an RTL bus working route 36 from Hither Green Station to West Kilburn Falcon. There is an interesting array of street furniture to the right of the bus. The canvas hut is for the policeman who controlled the traffic lights, and in front of him is a section box, these were installed at half mile intervals and fed 550/600 volts DC into the tramway. D.A.Thompson

In the newspaper columns devoted to readers' letters, the redoubtable A. E. Southernwood, a self-appointed champion of the tramways, was expressing his opinion. Under the heading *Time and Motion* he stated that tram crews should receive extra pay for punctuality. He lamented the fact that at Camberwell Green, he often saw half a dozen trams held up because the front car was waiting for a new crew. He then went on to say that if the new crew didn't arrive, the

car would be taken out of service, which resulted in a gap of fifteen minutes between two cars on that route. Appropriately, Mr Southernwood lived at Champion Hill, SE5.

The PW department was very active in February 1949. This may have been in response to local authority criticisms of the state of the track and more importantly the unevenness of the surrounding paving. LT had a statutory obligation to maintain the road surface between the rails and to a distance of 18in (458mm) either side of single track. Tracks were relaid on the Victoria Embankment east of Waterloo Bridge, and repairs were effected in the following thoroughfares: Westminster Bridge Road, Theobalds Road, Clapham Road and Clapham Common South Side.

March arrived with a fatal blow for tramway supporters, when on the fourth of the month, Lord Latham, Chairman of the London Transport Executive, outlined plans for the tramway conversion programme. The scheme proposed withdrawal of trams in nine stages, working west to east, thereby

leaving the CRD at Charlton to continue working until the end of routes 36 and 38 at stage nine. Lord Latham's speech included the following statements:

'While this conversion cannot be carried out until we have the necessary additional buses, about 1,100, there is much preliminary work to be done. Meantime we must keep the trams going at a very heavy and growing annual cost. The loss on the trams is about £1,000,000 a year. Now that we have Government sanction, we can get on with the building of two new garages and the alteration of seven of the existing tram depots required to handle the buses. The two new garages to be built are Stockwell and Rye Lane, Peckham. Tram depots which are to be converted are Wandsworth, Clapham, Camberwell, Thornton Heath, Streatham, New Cross and Abbey Wood. In each of the nine stages there will be an overnight change, trams one night, buses first thing next morning. Each stage will involve a batch of about 100 new buses. The cost of the conversion will be nearly £10,000,000.'

He continued to describe in detail the areas affected by the conversion, and went on to point out that replacement bus services would run over similar routes to existing tram routes, but would be allocated different route numbers to avoid confusion with the existing bus system.

From the Chairman's statement it was apparent that no further use was to be made of Purley and Norwood depots. The position of Charlton Works seemed to be secure as trolleybus overhauls would now be their *raison d'etre*. Although the clouds were also gathering in this direction, as the *Sunday Times* reported on 6th March that the trolleybus system was going to be scrapped.

Reaction to the tram replacement news was generally favourable by the travelling public. Additionally, all of the official sources seemed to have fallen in line with the decision, and Sir Cyril Hurcomb, Chairman of the British Transport Commission, advised the Minister of Transport of the 'high priority' of tram replacement. Sir Cyril was quoted as saying that maintenance of vehicles and tracks was costing around one and a half million pounds a year. The theme was taken up later next month, when on 16th May in the House of Commons, Mr Callaghan, the Parliamentary Secretary to the Minister of Transport, reiterated that the Government did not favour retaining systems which required keeping a fixed track in the public road.

Permanent way renewals during the month included the outer curve at Blackfriars which was relaid, but on the debit side, the Clapham South turning loop was discon-

nected. Spring arrived in the capital with commencement of the reconstruction of Creek Bridge, Deptford. A temporary bridge, with a single lifting span, was placed south of the existing bridge. The new structure contained double conduit tracks for routes 68 and 70. Sharp curves were a feature of the approach rails to the temporary bridge. As it turned out, trams were never to use the replacement Creek Bridge, as the temporary one was still in use in July 1951, when routes 68 and 70 breathed their last. Starting from 13th April, several service changes

Above Outside Brixton Hill Depot members of the PW department are hard at work trying to repair track and road paving, whilst at the same time ensuring free passage for the frequent tram service. No fewer than 11 men, all wearing flat hats, are engaged with hand tools and welding equipment. In many respects the maintenance of London's tram tracks was a dying art and it became increasingly difficult to recruit new personnel. A.B.Cross

Below The date is 10th July 1949 and the photographer has positioned himself on the west side of Creek Bridge in anticipation of the arrival of the first tram to use the new, temporary, structure. Cars 584 and 1170 rumble forward in the direction of Greenwich. J.H.Meredith

Above A couple of LT officials on the back platform are the only clue to the fact that Car 553 is the first service tram to cross the temporary lifting bridge over Deptford Creek. Well may the workmen stand back to admire the results of their labours – the new conduit tracks have been laid with precision and a high degree of engineering competence. J.H.Meredith

Right On 3rd July 1949, the Southern Counties Touring Society hired Car 1. Each tour participant had to fork out seven shillings and sixpence for the privilege of riding on this special tram. The SCTS was founded in 1947 and its driving force was William Crawforth. Some of the five London tours were captured on 9.5mm film by Geoffrey Ashwell. Car 1 is depicted at Lewisham Clock Tower on tracks normally used by routes 46 and 72. J.H.Meredith

took place. Route 44 had its peak hour, Monday to Friday, frequency increased by three trams. These replaced cars operating as extras on route 46 between Beresford Square and Eltham Church. Route 54 also suffered a peak hour reduction between Catford and Grove Park, compensated by an extension of route 74 from Downham to Grove Park.

The Light Railway Transport League was a nationwide society devoted to improving and modernising tramways; it still exists, having metamorphosed into the LRTA. It published a monthly magazine entitled *Modern Tramway*. Forty members of the LRTL opened May in sparkling style, when Feltham Car 2094 was hired for a special tour. It was noted that this particular car was resplendent in fresh paint and in excellent mechanical condition, having recently passed through Charlton Works. Chief Inspector Perry was 'on the handles', and he drove Car 2094 from Victoria to Southcroft Road. Tour participants were then transported to Purley, before returning to Victoria. The journey from Purley to Victoria was timed at 55 minutes. Perhaps many of the 40 members realised that an era of stability was about to end, for on 8th June space was made free in Wandsworth and Clapham depots to allow construction of garage facilities for diesel buses. This work would include filling tramway inspection pits, pro-

viding new bus docking pits, sinking fuel oil storage tanks in the ground and installing fuelling points. The old tramway traversers which were used to shift trams sideways, would also go. It was indeed the beginning of the end, and a tangible sign that progress towards the inevitable extinction of electric traction was now unstoppable.

Modern Tramway for July 1949 contained a number of details under the headline 'London Depot Changes'. According to the correspondent, Wandsworth Depot had been converted to overhead wire and a change pit constructed at the entrance. Removal of the conduit equipment within the depot made for an easier and safer conversion. Fleet changes included seventeen cars of the 1700 series E/1 which were shifted to Clapham Depot to work route 26. Fifty-one other E/1s were transferred from Clapham to Camberwell and New Cross. The 1500 series E/1 cars were now mostly stabled at New Cross. Six E/3 cars were moved from Thornton Heath to Norwood, which also received some rehabs from New Cross. Route 34 was now worked by Camberwell Depot and was operated mainly by E/3 cars, with the odd HR/2 and E/1 taking a turn. New Cross took over route 66 from Camberwell; Norwood worked most of route 10, although Telford Avenue still supplied one Feltham for this route. Telford Avenue took over Clapham's share of route 10 and part of the allocation of cars on routes 22 and 24. This latter transfer brought Felthams their last route conquest.

The summer of 1949 saw work continuing on the conversion scheme, but on 17th July, to counteract the gloom of abandonment, trams started using the temporary Creek Bridge in a westbound direction. Monday, 1st August was a Bank Holiday, and trams working routes 2/4, 8/20, 10, 16/18, 34 and 66 were subject to timetable alterations. It is interesting to observe that in spite of this 'reduced' service, the interval between route 2/4 trams on August Bank Holiday was still 2-3 minutes, and on the 34 from Chelsea to Blackfriars it was an unhurried 8 minutes! Two days later, new terminal arrangements came into operation at Victoria. The original loading island outside the Windsor Castle PH continued to be used by services 8, 20, 28 and 78. Drivers of cars on routes 8 and 20 were encouraged where possible to pick up passengers at the extreme end of the track, whilst routes 28 and 78 were to use a more forward position. The new passenger island outside Denison House, some yards short of

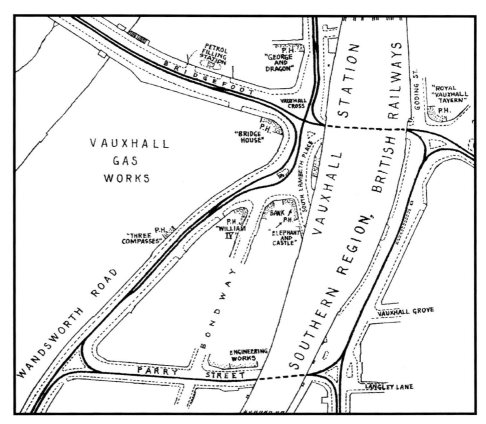

the terminal stub, now acted as the loading point for services 54, 58 and 66. Tram drivers on routes 54 and 66 were asked to use the forward part of the new island. All cars using the new facility had to reverse on the southernmost crossover, opposite 310/312 Vauxhall Bridge Road. The arrangement worked well, and with five trams loading simultaneously amongst a peak hour flow of 87 reversals an hour, the loading of

The alterations to the terminal arrangements at Victoria have caused the driver of Car 2046 to place his charge right near the end of the track by Little Big Ben. A London Transport banner supported by two concrete posts directs passengers to the southern loading island.
G.E.Baddeley

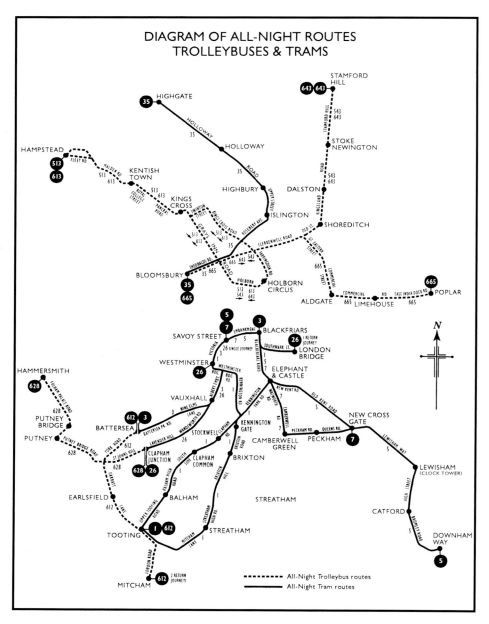

DIAGRAM OF ALL-NIGHT ROUTES TROLLEYBUSES & TRAMS

HIGHGATE
35
HAMPSTEAD
513
613
KENTISH TOWN
KINGS CROSS
HOLLOWAY
HIGHBURY
HOLLOWAY
ISLINGTON
STAMFORD HILL
643 643
STOKE NEWINGTON
DALSTON
SHOREDITCH
BLOOMSBURY
35 665
35
665
HOLBORN CIRCUS
ALDGATE
LIMEHOUSE
POPLAR
665

N

SAVOY STREET
5
7
3
BLACKFRIARS
26
LONDON BRIDGE
WESTMINSTER
26
ELEPHANT & CASTLE
HAMMERSMITH
628
PUTNEY BRIDGE
PUTNEY
VAUXHALL
612 3
BATTERSEA
STOCKWELL
KENNINGTON GATE
CAMBERWELL GREEN
PECKHAM
NEW CROSS GATE
7
CLAPHAM JUNCTION
628 26
CLAPHAM COMMON
BRIXTON
LEWISHAM (CLOCK TOWER)
EARLSFIELD
BALHAM
STREATHAM
CATFORD
TOOTING
1 612
STREATHAM
DOWNHAM WAY
5
MITCHAM
612
2 RETURN JOURNEYS

- - - - - All-Night Trolleybus routes
————— All-Night Tram routes

---

each car only took about 90 seconds! That London Transport should have invested in these passenger safety facilities so late in the day was at least commendable. The other side of the coin was that, with the increase of motor traffic, more and more passengers were taking their lives in their hands whilst stepping out in the carriageway to board a tramcar.

An interesting snippet of information was to be found in the October issue of *Modern Tramway*. The time card of a route 33 car, in service position 5, was quoted:

Depart from Holloway Depot at 3.32am.

Proceed to Angel, Manor House, Bloomsbury, Manor House.

Seven round trips: Manor House to West Norwood.

Manor House to Westminster.

Westminster to Highgate (as route 35), Highgate to Westminster, Westminster to Highgate, Highgate to Holloway Depot, arrive 12.42am.

The continuous running time was 21 hours 10 minutes, and it was claimed with some justification that this sort of performance could not be matched by the bus or

trolleybus departments. There seemed to be official concern about any layover period for tram crews, and in the September Traffic Circular, staff working route 34 were reminded of the regulations concerning trams at Beaufort Street, Chelsea terminus:

'The standing shall be for one tramcar, commencing at a point in line with the south-eastern building line of Alexandra Mansions and extending north-westward. Should a second tramcar arrive at the standing, the first tramcar is to proceed on its journey.'

Over on the other side of town, in Greenwich Church Street, similar instructions went out to crews:

'The standing shall be for two tramcars, commencing at a point opposite the entrance to No. 3 Greenwich Church Street and extending northward. Should a third tramcar arrive at the standing, the first tramcar is to proceed on its journey.'

Both of these instructions were part of a traffic control document drawn up by the Metropolitan Police. The fact that these two examples were topical in late 1949 may be due to complaints from residents and motorists, many of whom objected to the whole idea of on-street termini for trams.

Service alterations, effective from 19th October, marked a reduction in the frequency of cars on routes 2/4 from Wimbledon to the Embankment. All route 74 cars now worked a daily service to Grove Park. Peak hour and Saturday morning journeys on route 6 were cut back from Amen Corner, Tooting to Marius Road, Balham. However, these cuts were short lived, as on 2nd November the service was reinstated as far as Tooting Broadway. On 23rd November, there were some peak hour tram reallocations on services 8/20, 16/18 and 22/24, whereby Brixton Hill Depot gained nine trams at the expense of the nearby Telford Avenue Depot. As well as trams moving depot, there was a significant development involving a move over a much longer distance. In October 1949, Feltham Car 2099 was sent north to Leeds, so that it could take part in extended trials, before Leeds City Council ordered the purchase of the remaining UCC type trams. Car 2099 received a very favourable welcome and it was noted that its riding qualities over stretches of Leeds' reserved tracks were superb. Ironically, it was always intended by the old LUT that Feltham cars would run on new segregated tracks along the Uxbridge Road. Car 2099 retained its London fleet number until August 1950 when it was renumbered as Leeds Car 501.

Whilst the management at 55 Broadway was advertising its surplus wares up north, back on home ground enough progress had

Above The 'no more than two tramcars in Greenwich, Church Street' rule is about to be broken if they don't get Car 552 out of its predicament. In a classic crossover mess up it has split the points — one truck has sheared off towards the left. In theory this wasn't such a catastrophe, but one suspects that the plough may have been damaged by this unorthodox behaviour. At any rate the crew and curious bystanders look on. No doubt assistance from either New Cross or Charlton will arrive shortly. F.W.Ivey

Right Appropriately for the year in question, Car 1949 turns from Downham Way on to Bromley Road. It is working route 74 from Grove Park; the service interval on this route was a tram every six to eight minutes on weekdays. J.H.Meredith

been made in depot conversions to merit an article in the November issue of the *London Transport Magazine*, entitled *An Intricate Job*. It reassured readers that everything was going to plan and that: 'at Wandsworth, a joint tram-trolleybus depot, trolleybuses run quietly in and out of the depot at one side, trams are cleaned and inspected in the centre, and workmen are busy filling in and concreting the pits no longer required.' The

article was illustrated with suitable views of concrete mixers, piles of rubble, stacks of bricks, and trams using the new temporary overhead wires. In the case of Wandsworth, the trolleybuses were also receiving their marching orders, and route 612 would perish with tram route 12, to be replaced by bus route 44.

Left We encounter Car 1312 on route 20. The motorman is looking ahead to see there are no other trams approaching on the single track in Mitcham Lane. Babington Road leads off to the right. Had the pre-war South London trolleybus plans taken effect, this back street would have been the site of the Streatham turning loop.

Below Kennington Gate was one of those places where a tramway enthusiast could just stand and watch cars go by. The Horns Tavern on the corner of Kennington Road is in the centre of the picture opposite the third tram. On the right of the picture by the boundary of Kennington Park is a canvas hut for the pointsman. D.A.Thompson

The December issue of the magazine highlighted the work of Messrs A. Pedley, L. E. Venning and E. Usherwood, who formed one of the 12 New Cross teams which worked four snow brooms. Each snow broom was usually manned by a team of three, who had to turn out at any time of the day or night. Their job quite simply was to maintain the service by sweeping the tracks clear.

In those days, tram services were still operated on Christmas Day, although at a very reduced level. All-night routes for Christmas Eve and Christmas Night did not run, nor did trams on routes 6, 22, 24, 44, 52, 60, 62 and 84. Christmas Day service for route 46, to cite an example, began with an early journey at 4.30am from Abbey Wood to Eltham Church. The morning service interval was 10 minutes and that for the afternoon 8 minutes. The last car of the day left Beresford Square at 3.14pm and arrived at New Cross Depot at 3.56pm. Other route alterations were as follows:

2 – Clapham Junction, *Falcon* to Victoria Embankment, *Savoy Street*.

40 – Woolwich, *Beresford Square* to Victoria Embankment, *Savoy Street*.

48 – West Norwood, *Thurlow Arms* to Elephant and Castle.

72 – Woolwich, *Beresford Square* to New Cross Gate.

A newspaper report, dated 30th December, confirmed that rebuilding of Telford Avenue Depot had commenced. Of the two car sheds, the smaller one had been demolished; the boundary between the two sheds was marked by a Metropolitan Water Board main which connected to a nearby reservoir. This feature had to be diverted into a new tunnel under the new bus garage. Thirty

Coldharbour Lane, Brixton on a gloomy day, with E/3 Car 164 slowing for a compulsory stop. Above the tram is a skate in the overhead which, when activated by a trolley wheel, will send the appropriate signal to the nearby traffic lights. On receiving the green light, Car 164 will then swing into Gresham Road, behind where the photographer is standing. N.Rayfield

men were employed on demolition and twelve on construction work. The report finished by adding that work was about to start on garages at Stockwell for 200 buses, and at Peckham for 125 buses.

Such was 1949 for the trams and their long suffering crews. The start of the second half of the twentieth century would bring a welcome boost to national morale as preparations for the Festival of Britain got under way. It would also see the commencement of the post-war tramway abandonment programme.

CAMPAIGN TO SAVE THE SYSTEM

IN RETROSPECT it is obvious that the campaign to save London's first generation tramway system was doomed to failure. It became an impossible task to alter the entrenched views of London Transport and the national government. Also ranged against the trams were an array of pressure groups, most prominent of which were motoring organisations. These bodies also had the tacit support of the bus manufacturers and town planners whose only vision for the future lay bound in with the concept of 'flexibility' for the provision of public transport. Another drawback was that tramways never had the appeal of steam railways or the international mystique of ocean liners. Most folk simply regarded them as a humdrum part of everyday life, and their replacement by a more 'modern' form of transport was seen as part of the natural order of things. However, there were those who felt differently, and in November 1937 the Light Railway Transport League was founded in London by J. W Fowler. His aims were quite straightforward: the modernisa-

tion and retention of electric tramways. In pursuit of extra publicity for the cause, Fowler organised the famous trip on 15th May 1938, when car 1 was hired to transport enthusiasts from Waltham Cross to Purley – then the longest tram journey one could make in London. This gathering together of the like minded prompted debate as to mounting a campaign to save the remainder of the London system.

Opinions were divided. There were those who favoured a direct 'hands on' approach to influence LT policy, and others who gave general support but were not willing to engage in activities like holding public meetings, distributing leaflets and writing to the newspapers. A third group of members were more interested in history and looked with nostalgia on past glories. Inevitably this meant that the campaigning strength of the LRTL was diluted and this remained the case when the fight to save London's tramways began again after the Second World War. On the credit side, shortly before the outbreak of hostilities, a small band of

members commenced a study of South London tramway facilities, where roads and tram routes were surveyed. The information was then used to draw up modernisation plans which included reserved tracks and passenger loading islands. Needless to say, when this document was submitted to London Transport, it sank without trace. Lord Ashfield, Frank Pick, Sir Henry Maybury and the other board members were firmly convinced that the sooner they got rid of the trams the better.

As has been suggested previously, there was a 'class element' in the movement to scrap the trams. Many of those people who had wealth and influence still regarded the tram as a vehicle for the working class. A vehicle, furthermore, which got in the way of their desires to exploit the 'open road' in their motor cars. The trolleybus was only tolerated as a replacement, so long as it didn't get anywhere near the more select areas of the capital, where peers and dukes of the realm, and residents of exclusive London squares held court. Sadly, this particular

Left Natural traffic corridors like the Old Kent Road seemed most fitted for continued tramway operation. Tracks could have been moved on to reservation or, as a transition measure, loading islands could have been provided to protect passengers. However, the powers that be were not of a mind to carry out any of these progressive steps, and the upgrade to rapid transit never occurred. Many years after the demise of the trams, dedicated bus lanes were constructed for the allegedly 'more flexible' form of transport, but by then, most traffic had slowed to a crawl and the buses just joined in to increase pollution levels. D.A. Thompson

Below The trams were targeted by several newspapers in a campaign to convince readers that they were inherently unsafe. As we now know, the great improvement in London street accident statistics, which was promised after the departure of the trams, never happened and the death toll kept on rising. One hopes Road Safety Week in Islington did get its message across. In the intervening years after this photograph was taken, the junction of Upper Street and Essex Road has become somewhat more dangerous, especially for pedestrians and cyclists. D.A. Thompson

British obsession with class, accent and birthright also partly infected the LRTL, which was regarded by many tramway workers as rather middle class. A conductor from New Cross Depot related how several participants on a League tour had expressed support for those 'volunteers' who drove trams during the 1926 General Strike. The conductor, a Transport and General Workers Union stalwart, was quick to point out to these 'tramway amateurs' that they had never known what it was like to struggle for a living. He then shocked the little group by saying what he and his fellow workers would have done to the 1926 blacklegs!

Although there was a genuine affection for tramways amongst many LT employees, it is safe to say that the attitude of LT, the Labour Government and the TGWU was fairly consistent. New and better road vehicles, in the form of the RT bus, would provide a flexible, more integrated service – thus in this sense, the post-war abandonment programme was never a party political issue. It was the consensus of transport experts that trams had had their day. Argu-

ments such as the danger of relying on imported oil and rubber found little support in the corridors of power. As for the growth of motor vehicles, it was confidently predicted that the average speed of London's traffic would increase after the removal of the trams. Parking was not foreseen as a problem, and the use of American style parking meters was discounted as unBritish! Concerns about pollution mainly centred on burning smokeless fuels, which would ease the fog situation. The possible harmful effects of exhaust fumes from the thousand or so new buses were given the same short shrift as American parking meters.

In spite of all these institutional hurdles the campaign to save the trams did attract some talented individuals. Many regarded C. R. Bizeray's book *Towards Ideal Transport*, first published in 1944, as an inspiration to counteract the ideas of Abercrombie and Forshaw. Bizeray was tragically killed before the post-war campaign got under way, but his vision of an integrated transport system, where trams would use reserved tracks and city centre subways, lived on. Indeed, the

Kingsway Subway and the Victoria Embankment seemed to offer a perfect example of what could be achieved; these tracks could form the basis of a new rapid transit system. The use of this American phrase was no accident. It was across the Atlantic that enthusiasts looked for their inspiration, mainly to the PCC streetcar which embodied all the notions of modern electric traction.

The PCC car was a revolutionary vehicle – a streamlined, single deck tramcar which rode on superbly engineered trucks, giving a quiet and comfortable ride. When, on 1st October 1936, Mayor Fiorello H. La Guardia of New York, inaugurated service of Brooklyn and Queens Transit Car 1009, a new era

in rail transportation opened. Orders followed from American and Canadian cities and eventually almost 5,000 cars rolled off the production line. This figure was augmented by the 15,000 PCC cars or vehicles built under PCC patents which appeared in Europe and Asia. The concession for England was snapped up by Crompton-Parkinson. They produced an advanced VAMBAC system (Variable Automatic Multinotch Braking and Acceleration Control), compatible with PCC technology, and 42 sets of equipment were used by London Underground in the late 1930s. In 1937, W Vane Morland, the Leeds manager, visited Boston to see the new design. He then returned home with the blueprints of the PCC, but the outbreak of war put paid to any more progress.

Tramway preservationists envisaged a fleet of single ended cars which, if need be, could be run as coupled pairs. Single ended cars needed loops or reversing triangles, such as used by steam tram and trailer sets. These proposed new vehicles could be accommodated on the London network, especially as the Embankment formed part of a large loop terminus. This type of PCC could then operate on the Tooting and Streatham 'circles' and on routes from Eltham which terminated at Beresford Square. Even the humble route 44 could circumnavigate the roundabout at Middle Park Avenue by the

insertion of a small section of connecting track. As it was, the nearest LT got to espousing the PCC cause was an article in the July 1948 issue of *London Transport Magazine*.

Bearing in mind the number of fact finding missions by LT excutives to observe public transport in other countries and cities where trams still held sway, it becomes increasingly obvious that closed minds were the order of the day. Interestingly, in the 1948 article, no mention was made by the author of the numbers of PCC cars which operated in Washington DC on the conduit system. The enthusiast-activists hadn't missed this one, and it seemed a golden opportunity to prove that even the much maligned conduit might have a future. Letters were sent to 55 Broadway offering LT the chance to try out a modern tram at the LRTL's expense.

There were two possible candidates to offer on trial – Blackpool car 208 and Glasgow car 1005. Both vehicles were equipped with up-to-date VAMBAC electronic control, which promised smoother starting and braking, thus allowing higher schedule speeds with safety and comfort for passengers. In addition the trucks were fitted with improved motors, and more importantly, resilient wheels which gave a much quieter ride. Both cars presented a stark contrast to traditional London tramcar design practices.

Above Double deck traditionalists had their eyes on Glasgow for inspiration. Car 1005 is a sleek, streamlined tramcar mounted on PCC type trucks. What impression it might have caused in the capital is a matter of conjecture, but compared to a standard RT bus, the Glasgow design looks very futuristic. B.J.Cross

Below Blackpool car 208 was the one serious candidate that LRTL members were willing to have transported to London. Note the PCC trucks which were far superior to anything London Transport possessed. B.J.Cross

The Blackpool car was a standard gauge, single decker with centre entrance/exit; it had a conventional trolley pole, and could probably have performed well on the Streatham to Purley section. The Glasgow car was a 'one off', uni-directional double decker. Car 1005 has been called the only double deck PCC car ever built, and it was certainly an eye opener, appearing as it did in a smart livery of three shades of blue. However, three factors ruled out its operation in the capital. Single ended cars need turning loops, and the only overhead wire route in London which could accommodate Car 1005 was the section between Beresford Square and Well Hall Roundabout. Glasgow trams used bow collectors instead of trolley poles. In pre-war days the LCC had wired the Grove Park to Downham line for both trolleys and bows/pantographs, but in the meantime many of the fittings had been replaced. Finally, the Glasgow track gauge was three quarters of an inch (19mm) narrower than standard gauge.

It seemed logical that, with the Festival of Britain on the horizon, the Operating Manager (Trams and Trolleybuses) might just be persuaded to change his mind and accept Blackpool 208. The reponse was in the negative and the Public Relations department replied to the LRTL in a letter dated 23rd March 1950. It included the following statements:

'Work on the replacement of the remaining trams is proceeding rapidly, and it is expected that the first stage of the conversion scheme will be completed before the end of the year, and that the scheme as a whole will be finished within a period of three years. You will see, therefore, that the Executive are committed to a policy of substituting oil-engined buses for the tramway system, a policy which they consider to be right and proper. In these circumstances the Executive regret that they cannot avail themselves of the offer you have made.'

The London area group of the LRTL was still pressing its case, and the name of Alan Watkins, Chairman of the South London Committee, came to the fore. Alan was a tireless campaigner for what he perceived as a just cause. Although the doors of 55 Broadway were firmly shut, he, like many others, found a forum in the letters columns of London's weekly and evening newspapers. An extract from a letter he wrote to the Editor of *The Star* gives an insight into contemporary arguments for tramway retention (*The Star* was one of a trio of London evening papers which also included the *Evening News* and the *Evening Standard*):

'The evidence given at the Transport Tribunal has made it clear that the conversion scheme has considerably influenced the fare proposals. Although the reason given is an intention to 'level' road and rail fares, it should be stressed that the bulk, if not all, of the increased revenue (£2½ to £3½ million) will go to a concern already making a profit. Rail single fares will, in some cases, be reduced, but day return tickets do not appear to be altered (e.g. Bexley to Charing Cross will remain at two shillings and tenpence), and most people use return tickets.

It is therefore reasonable to assume that the increase is to pay for the tramway conversion scheme, and this has been partially admitted. It is also verified by the fact that, in most large towns to scrap trams, fares have risen considerably, as witness the following examples:

Manchester.
Trams gone and fares still rising.

Liverpool.
Fares rise and cheap facilities are withdrawn as each tram route is closed.

London.
There have been two fare increases tramway abandonment commenced.

'Witnesses at the Transport Tribunal have suggested that tramway modernisation would remove the necessity for such heavy fare increases, and certain figures were published in *The Star* recently. It should be stessed that heavy capital expenditure over a short period is an economic necessity with the bus programme, but the expenditure on a tramway modernisation programme could be spread over a period, as much of the existing equipment could be used. It has been

suggested that London's trams are on their last legs, but while this is true of some, it is not true of the whole fleet. Ninety-two trams are to be sold to another authority, and about 200 others may also be sold. Transport authorities would not buy old junk! An improved standard of maintenance would eliminate the present uncomfortable riding and breakdowns . . .

'Another aspect is that of fuel and rubber. Both buses and trolleybuses use rubber, and buses imported diesel oil . . . In view of the economic situation it is necessary to curtail imports to a minimum, and the increased use of trams, and to a lesser extent trolleybuses, would help in this direction.'

Alan Watkins' energies were also directed to the organisation of public meetings, liaison with the press, and the distribution of pro-tram leaflets and circulars. His work was complemented by the efforts of other prominent activists such as Julian Thompson, John Walton and Gerald Druce. The local newspapers of most value in getting the message across were the *South London Press*, *South London Observer*, and *Brixton Free Press*; other papers which occasionally carried tramway matter were the *Kentish Messenger* and the *Balham, Tooting and Mitcham News*.

Public meetings were held at Brixton, Streatham, Lewisham and Eltham. Attendance at these gatherings varied from a successful meeting on 25th March 1950 at St Leonard's Church Hall, Streatham, which pulled in 80–100 people, to a poor showing of

only a handful of members on 4th November at a South-eastern group meeting in Progress Hall, Eltham. The Streatham meeting and a subsequent one held on 15th June at Lambeth Town Hall, were addressed by Messrs Farrell and Horn, who employed film strip projector illustrations of modern cars and track layouts to augment their speeches. Alan Watkins also spoke on the proposed use of modern tramways in the Brixton area. Both gatherings recorded a sympathetic reaction from members of the public and resolutions were passed to urge LT to suspend the scrapping programme pending experiments with modern tramcars.

Leaflet distribution was carried out by volunteers and some thousands of circulars against the tramway conversion programme were delivered in an organised house-to-house campaign. An eight-man group called the Tramway Development Council was formed. Its headquarters were in Peckham, and its spokesman, S. P. Harris, outlined ideas for new trams, segregated tracks and better traffic flows. This devotion to the cause was remarkable, as fellow enthusiast Julian Thompson notes in his diary for 3rd June 1950:

In the afternoon we went to Camberwell, where a depot visit had been arranged for active South London LRTL members by Mr Barrie. The whole of the depot was visited, and it was a very interesting two hours, ending with tea in the canteen. Later we spent two and a half hours distributing Brixton Public Meeting leaflets in the Clapham area.

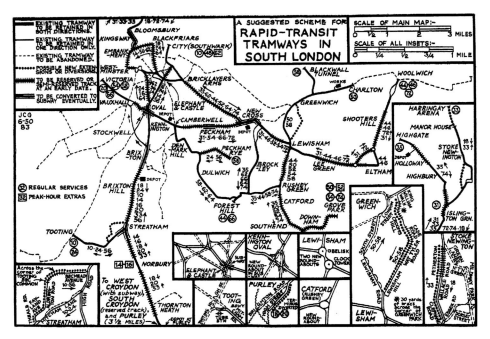

In the July 1950 issue of *Modern Tramway*, there appeared an article by E K. Farrell, entitled *A Future for London's Tramways: A Practical Scheme*. It was touted as a short term programme, in advance of a more substantial conversion of existing street tramways into rapid transit lines, such as were beginning to be constructed in Germany and other continental countries. But in reality the whole text seems like an eleventh hour attempt at a rescue act for what remained of the tramways. Another activist, David H. Refoy, an LRTL member, had already submitted some ideas for the construction of reserved track tramways along the arterial roads envisaged in the *County of London Plan*, and some of this material was combined with the Farrell scheme. The whole effort was ingenious and it is worth quoting in detail the proposals for a revamped system.

The article sets its aim as the retention of only the most suitable tramways for modernisation, i.e. those lines which could be operated as an express service to compensate for the lack of a comprehensive tube railway system in the areas served. It also enumerates further criteria, such as abandonment of those lines confined to narrow streets, or those routes with insufficient passengers. Right from the start overhead wires were to be erected in place of the conduit, cars would then be converted from trolley pole current collection to either bow or pantograph. This, together with improved track and junction layouts, would enable higher service speeds. The only exception to the all overhead plan

might be the Kingsway Subway, Victoria Embankment and its approaches, where the conduit would be retained for aesthetic and practical reasons.

The routes centred on Wandsworth Depot were not considered viable, mainly because they represented the rump of the pre-war system, part of which had been turned over to trolleybuses. Neither was the trunk route from the Oval to Wimbledon deemed worthy of retention. The argument here being that this stretch was already paralleled by the Northern Line tube. A similar reason was advanced for the sacrifice of the Charlton–Woolwich–Abbey Wood section, because it ran near an electrified suburban line operated by Southern Region. The remaining services, totalling about 65 route miles (104km), would have an average of three stops per mile, and all stops would be provided with loading islands.

A glance at John Gillham's map, above, will give route locations. It will be noted that the whole scheme was based on the then existing lines. New routes across London were not contemplated, at least not at this stage of planning. With the benefit of hindsight one can see considerable drawbacks to the proposals. Although one could perhaps justify the retention of service 58 because of high passenger loadings, the inclusion of the Peckham Rye branch, and its reconstruction on reserved track, seems overly optimistic. Other termini such as Blackwall Tunnel and Charlton also seem to fly in the face of logic, but the creators of this plan weren't to know the London traffic flows of the future, which

would see such an important tramway thoroughfare as the Victoria Embankment become almost a public transport free zone! Gridlock, vast one way schemes, pollution, no parking spaces, traffic wardens, wheel clamping, road rage, double yellow lines and red routes were unforeseen nightmares for the coming decades.

Aside from geographical constraints, the vexed subject of the type of tram needed to service the new network caused some debate. Ironically the LCC may have actually got it right when it opened the Kingsway Subway for single deck cars, and to many forward thinking enthusiasts the double deck concept was a dead duck. The single *versus* double deck debate was to rumble on way past the final abandonment of London's trams, and the LRTL was not to know in 1950 that one person operation, plus significant technical developments in tramcar construction in Germany and other European countries, would render the double deck tramcar obsolete.

It was assumed that the sale of the Felthams to Leeds could not be halted, and so attention should be concentrated on a post-war reconditioning programme involving E/1 and E/3 cars. The HR/2 class vehicles were to be scrapped, to be replaced 'by completely new cars, of a type which would by this time be ascertained by experiment'. The choice between single deck and double deck, it was pointed out, was not as easy to make as might at first be thought, and to be considered were the three subways suggested by the Tramway Development Council's scheme for the Purley line, which rendered single deckers desirable in that case. The article continues to describe other reasons for operating at least some single deckers, especially single ended, single deck cars coupled back to back in pairs. It was estimated that these vehicles could use existing depot facilities, provided they were uncoupled before being shifted about on the depot traversers. The whole scheme was costed at around £3.5 million, which certainly looked better value than LT's £10 million bus conversion plan, or the £20 million it would take to build only one tube extension to either Grove Park or Croydon.

In all fairness this LRTL sponsored scheme was a brave attempt to salvage something from the wreckage. It was submitted to London Transport. We shall never know if it raised any eyebrows at 55 Broadway. The bright new vision worked out by Mr Farrell and his colleagues was probably placed in a filing cabinet with a note marked NO ACTION pinned to it!

In order to bolster the establishment case further, Sir Cyril Hurcomb gave this reply to LRTL criticisms:

'The decision to replace the South London trams by oil engined buses was taken only after the most careful and prolonged consideration of the alternatives. The use of buses will make it possible to effect better co-ordination with existing bus routes, including the extension of routes to serve better traffic objectives, while the retention in service of the trams would create grave problems. An expansion in capacity of the electricity distribution system would be necessary and additional sub stations would have to be constructed. A substantial expansion of the cable system would also be needed. Both electrical equipment and cables are in short supply and delivery dates are likely to be a long way ahead. The erection of trolley poles and overhead wires, as suggested in your letter, would have to include Westminster Bridge and the Embankments in close proximity to the Houses of Parliament, and would involve a serious lowering of civic amenity in the heart of the capital.'

Thus the debate continued up to and beyond the first tram route withrawals. The actual abandonment process commenced on 1st October 1950, and with each stage the mood of the activists became gloomier. Such arguments as loss of passenger capacity on the replacing buses seemed to cut no ice. Even fare increases and the loss of transfer and return fares failed to move sufficient numbers of the public to complain. And because public pressure on the issue was half-hearted, there was no incentive for politicians to take up the cause. The LRTL did try dabbling in the political pond when, in July 1951, it sent a delegation to meet members of the Conservative Party Research Committee on Transport. There was, it was reported, 'a full and frank discussion', but of course nothing of import ever came out of this meeting, nor out of a second meeting in March 1952. Other informal contacts with representatives of the electrical industry and local authorities also failed to provoke any meaningful action.

London Transport relied on public and government support for their actions, and it has to be said that the correspondence columns of local newspapers had their fair share of anti-tram propagandists, who were quite happy to see the departure of what they considered to be 'a railbound menace'. Many tram crews were looking forward to working on buses, and motormen in particular would now be able to sit down on the job for the first time. The task of tramway supporters became increasingly more difficult as the travelling public accepted the inevitable; many people actually liked the replacing buses, and said so to LT officials and the newspapers. The following letter, sent to the press in November 1949 was typical:

'Isn't it time the trams were removed from our streets completely? They are dangerous, inconvenient and slow. The slightest breakdown causes them to pile up in endless queues, leaving hundreds of work weary people stranded. And it would be interesting to know what percentage of road accidents are caused either by people jumping off them in the middle of the road (necessarily), or by other vehicles skidding on their damnable lines.'

Aside from the inveterate tram haters, the positive nature of bus route extensions into the West End past old tram termini also received a welcome. For example, passengers on route 45 could now reach South Kensington from Battersea, and were no longer hampered by the inconvenience of changing at Battersea Bridge or Beaufort Street.

As was said at the beginning of this chapter, the campaign was doomed to failure, but the activists, to their credit, did not give up until the end. On the last day, some took nostalgic last rides, but others like Alan Watkins were appalled by what they regarded as a criminal waste of resources. Alan spent Saturday, 5th July 1952, walking in solitary contemplation by the River Medway in Kent. All he had fought for had now gone.

THE DAWN of 1950 brought new hope to Londoners. It was an important psychological divide – hardship, war, destruction, austerity and the harsh winters of the 1940s seemed to belong to a more distant age. Prosperity was returning, and the advent of antibiotics, the National Health Service and new employment laws had begun to exorcise the scourges of disease and poverty which had characterised pre-war years. People could look forward to the future, and to the new showcase of British achievement, the Festival of Britain, which was due to open in 1951 on the South Bank opposite Victoria Embankment.

The trams were still running, and indeed the rumble of cars over Westminster Bridge had a deceptive air of permanence. But the reality of tramway abandonment was just round the corner, and the planners at London Transport intensified their efforts to complete the programme within the allotted time span.

January 1950 began with a flurry of activity. On New Year's Day, Thornton Heath Depot was closed and its trams moved south across Croydon to Purley Depot. Crew and depot staff stayed on to say farewell to car 382, the last to leave the depot. Shortly afterwards the whole site of the former Thornton Heath Depot was levelled and none of the original building was incorporated into the new bus garage. At Purley some minor changes were effected to the overhead wiring so as to come into line with its new status as a running shed. The official

instructions to tram crews warned drivers and conductors to exercise care to avoid accidents from overtaking vehicles when taking trams in or out of Purley Depot. It was further impressed on staff that drivers should be particularly vigilant when driving trams over the track giving access to the pits on the northern side of the depot. A speed limit of two miles per hour was enforced when passing the canteen and adjoining outbuildings.

The builders were also busy at Clapham where a large hole had been knocked in the back of the depot. At a patch of spare ground adjoining Penhall Road, Charlton, construction activity of another sort resulted in tram scrapping sidings being laid out. By mid-January a rail connection had been constructed from the scrapyard to the eastbound track in Woolwich Road. This Penhall Road spur became fully operational on 12th February, when London's last change pit was con-

Left The interior of Clapham Depot in 1950 with all its tramway fixtures and fittings, including the traverser in the middle of the picture, gives no clue as to the impending reconstruction works. Other features to note are the cleaners' gantries and the neat stack of side destination boards. F.Jones

Right A fine study in conduit trackwork reveals the new connection from Woolwich Road into Penhall Road yard. C.Carter

structed – a tram on its last journey would reverse in Woolwich Road on to the entrance track, then the trolley would be raised and the plough run out for the final time. The doomed car would then use its own power until it was shunted on to the yard traverser, to be placed on one of the storage tracks.

Clapham Depot was also in the news earlier in February when reconstruction work featured in a newspaper article:

'In Clapham only 28 trams are left of the 120 that used to be there. Half the space is already concreted over and the tram pits filled up to nine inches from the ground level, leaving only the rails to be taken up. Pits for buses are already partly constructed at Clapham, and a pit 25 feet deep has been dug for the tanks, holding 1,500 gallons of fuel oil. Capacity will be 150 buses, the first of which will roll out in October.'

The article goes on to describe the future course of events:

'Tram drivers have not yet started training as bus drivers, but all crews will be given the opportunity of switching over. Man in charge of all conversion work in South London is Mr W. Robertson. He is the link between London Transport and the various contractors engaged on the conversion scheme . . . When the day comes, the trams will go to the tram cemetery at Charlton, where after recovering plateglass and horse-hair, and shifting scrapped tracks to steel foundries, a pyre will be mark the graveyard of South London's trams.'

The last sentence of this report had somewhat garbled the facts, but it produced a reaction in some readers who deplored the fact that London's trams were going to the bonfire when so many people were without homes – 'let the public buy them and have them temporarily erected on bomb sites' was one of the sentiments expressed.

The London Transport publicity machine was also preparing for the changeover. It issued a statement that the arrival of some 250 new buses to take the place of the first four tram route casualties, would herald 'shorter queues and more comfort next winter. And for the people of Wandsworth, Clapham, Battersea and Vauxhall it means quicker travel as well.' However, before the grand switch-over the trams were still called upon to transport large numbers of people, especially during the morning and evening peak hours. Concerns were being expressed about the forthcoming change to buses and a heartfelt plea from one particular passenger was published in the evening press:

'Southwark workers who want to get to their homes in Camberwell or Brixton find that all trams and buses are full when they arrive at Stamford Street, and most have to wait until the Embankment rush has been cleared. This is most unfair and could be remedied by turning an occasional tram back at Stamford Street during the rush hour. It is amazing to see the patience of the people who, having secured shorter hours of work, have to waste many hours in the cold and often wet weather, without any shelter when it could be easily put right. I dread what will happen when our trams are taken off the road.'

Movement of homebound workers was only part of the trams' remit, they were also vital in shifting football supporters. On the occasion of the fourth-round FA cup tie, Chelsea *v* Newcastle, the frequency of service 34 cars from Kings Road was increased to 25 per hour; a tram left Beaufort Street terminus every two minutes after the final whistle. The situation at Charlton was handled just as well, where 46,000 fans who had seen the home side draw with Cardiff City, were treated to a service interval along the

Above Although trolleybus overhead at Wandsworth Depot was the norm, engineers erected tramway overhead for the last few months before buses took over. This enabled the conduit in the depot to be removed quickly and safely. Car 201 waits to shed its plough at the depot.
A.D.Packer

Below The fans are out in force in this scene in Woolwich Road by Charlton Church Lane. The Valley, home of Charlton Athletic FC, lies just round the corner, and thousands of supporters used to rely on the frequent tram service to get to and from the game. At the start of the 1952–53 football season, the chairman of Charlton Athletic complained to London Transport about the wholly inadequate bus service which could not cope with the crowds.
C.Carter

Above The date is 1st July 1950, and work on Stangate, the new street at the northern end of Lambeth Palace Road, is temporarily suspended for the photographer to complete his shot. We are looking west towards the war damaged St Thomas's Hospital. Note the specially milled girder rail which required a check rail to be bolted on.

Below North of Westminster Bridge Road lay Addington Street. Here, on 17th February 1950, we are looking east at the points leading to the Addington Street siding. This was the world's last section of new conduit track. J.H.Meredith

Woolwich Road of a tram every 65 seconds! After both matches the crowds were cleared within 45 minutes.

Throughout February, the preliminary works in connection with the Festival of Britain roundabout at County Hall were continuing. It was noted that, on a bombed site between Addington Street and Westminster Bridge Road, conduit track and points were taking shape. The opportunity of witnessing the construction of new conduit tracks was not lost on many enthusiasts, and the progress on this, London's last tramway extension, was subject to much scrutiny. Construction work of another kind had, by 14th February, lowered Wandsworth Depot's fleet strength to a mere 36 trams.

An upbeat note was sounded by a diary entry for 18th February, when Julian Thompson noted the appearance of Car 1 on route 20 at Trinity Road Station. This vehicle was always a favourite with tram fans, but, being non-standard, its use in latter days was confined to peak hours and the occasional enthusiasts' trips. These were organised by the Southern Counties Touring Society and the LRTL. The SCTS hired Car 1 for tours on 5th September 1948 and on 3rd July 1949. Although the car was fitted with similar equipment to the HR/2

class, London Transport would not allow its use on Dog Kennel Hill, which was regularly worked by HR/2s. The usual driver on the specials was Alf Perry, Chief Inspector at the Clapham Depot tramway training school. Mr Perry, aged 64, had begun his working life as an LCC fitter in 1906. The LRTL also used Car 1 on the last day of the Croydon routes on 7th April 1951.

An unforeseen structural alteration to London's tramways occurred on 17th March when Battersea Bridge was damaged by an errant coal barge. The bridge was closed to all vehicular traffic and the tracks carrying route 34 were effectively abandoned. Trams had to reverse at a crossover on the south side of the bridge. For the final months of service 34 cars showed LATCHMERE on the indicator blind. However, there was a silver lining. Until 7th June, extra trams were run to compensate for the loss of buses in Battersea Park Road, bus routes 19, 39 and 49 having been diverted via Chelsea Bridge. The last tram to leave Beaufort Street on the fateful night of 16th March was crewed by Messrs Ernest Spinner and William Mavir from Camberwell Depot.

It was reported during the month that the sojourn of Feltham Car 2099 in Leeds had been a successful one. Leeds City Council were minded to purchase the remaining 92 cars of type UCC at a price of £500 each. It was also confirmed that Torre Road Depot,

Leeds would be altered to accommodate the longer Feltham cars. This seemingly bright sign for transport in the Yorkshire city would be shortly overshadowed by a shift in political control on the council which resulted in a decision to scrap the trams. However, this change of heart was in the future when, on 2nd April, an LRTL party hired Car 2099 for a tour of the Leeds system. It was remarked that the riding qualities of the Feltham were first class, and that: 'The reconditioning of this car is a tribute to Leeds City Transport, and its appearance on most of the city's routes has created widespread interest and praise.'

Back in the capital city, April saw the eastbound track from Charing Cross to Savoy Street being relaid. This work may have been prompted by a derailment on 1st April, when a 36 tram held up the service along the Victoria Embankment for 20 minutes. On 5th April, there were breakdowns on Westminster Bridge and in Walworth Road, Camberwell, both of which caused delays and queues of waiting trams. On a more sombre note, the overhead in Penhall Road scrapyard was completed, and to all intents and purposes it was now ready to receive its unfortunate victims. Good Friday fell on 7th April, and the familiar pattern of route and timetable changes was applied for the Easter period.

The elements intervened on the night of

25th/26th April, when a heavy snow fall left treacherous driving conditions. Streets were covered to a depth of two inches, but tram tracks had been swept clear by snow brooms.

There were a number of alterations and fleet reallocations which were effective from 3rd May. Cars on routes 8, 20, 22 and 24 took part in a game of 'musical chairs' whereby some vehicles were shuffled in and out of Telford Avenue, Brixton Hill and Clapham depots. It was noted that some of the 1500 series E/1s had been transferred to Clapham. On the other side of town, shortworking cars on service 54 were extended from Catford to Downham, at the same time as the service frequency of route 72 was cut by three trams. Finally, some peak hour workings on route 70 were withdrawn between Bermondsey Street and Tooley Street. If the casual traveller wanted to find the exact location of Tooley Street, or indeed any other important thoroughfare traversed by the tramways, then he needed to look no further than the new LT *Trolleybus and Tram Map* which appeared during the month. In many ways it was a superb map with routes shown clearly. It maintained the LCC tradition of detailing service frequencies and the times of first and last trams.

Speculation about proposed fare rises was never far from the surface. Public relations people at LT preferred the expression 'fare adjustments', but whatever the terminology, it became increasingly obvious that it would be more expensive to ride on a bus or a tram. These changes were set to start on 1st October and included, amongst other things, the complete abolition of workmen's fares. On 7th March, F. K. Farrell wrote: 'The national press report that London Transport fares are to be increased next October to offset the cost of conversion from trams to buses.'

Local authorities and other organisations representing community interests were also concerned about the issue, and doubts were raised whether passengers would get a fair deal on the replacing buses. It was calculated that those who travelled to work in London would pay another £3½ million a year for transport. On 22nd March, the TUC joined in the fight and its Special Economic Committee broached the topic of the 4½ per cent fare rise in a meeting with Sir Stafford Cripps, the Chancellor of the Exchequer.

Elements opposed to fare increases found a suitable *cause célèbre* when it was alleged that 600,000 people who normally bought workmen's tickets would have to pay more. Lionel Heald KC, putting the BTC's case at an official enquiry, referred to workmen's tickets as an anachronism. He continued by saying that he did not think one class of traveller should be subsidised by another class of traveller, or by the taxpayer. It's unlikely that Mr Heald had the remotest idea what it was like to be on a restricted income and to be reliant on cheap tram fares to get to and from work. There was always a suspicion that the bus conversion scheme was costing more than the authorities let on, hence the increase in fares to fund it. This point was tackled by R. Reader Harris, Conservative MP for Heston and Isleworth. He pursued a spirited cross-examination of A. B. Valentine, Operating Manager of London Transport.

MR HARRIS (for the London Passengers Association): Isn't it a fact that you will have to have three buses to replace two trams?

MR VALENTINE: I think it is more like six buses to five trams, but there will be additional staff required.

MR HARRIS: Would it not be possible to postpone this scheme for a year or two to avoid the increases?

MR VALENTINE: It would be quite impossible to keep the trams running. They are on their last legs. At this stage it would be impossible to stop the scheme because much of the physical work, such as the conversion of tram depots to buses, has already been carried out.

MR HARRIS: You are absolutely satisfied that no economies could be made?

MR VALENTINE: That is not what I say to my staff, but the scope for dramatic economies is now very small.

A strong objection was also registered by P. Barnes, Secretary of the London Co-operative Society, who said he spoke for a million members who had agreed to protest against the abolition of workmen's fares. The tribunal dragged on into June, the high point being a moment of pure farce when Mr Harris tried to have Lord Latham and Sir Cyril Hurcomb forcibly brought to testify.

Mr Heald considered this a piece of impertinence, and the worthy chairman of the tribunal, Sir William Bruce Thomas KC, inclined to agree. R. Reader Harris MP was denied further access to the true state of affairs at 55 Broadway.

Whatever the merits of this argument over the state of transport finances, money was still being invested in the changeover and the first batch of motormen left Wandsworth on 12th June to begin retraining for diesel buses. They were soon followed by men from Clapham Depot. Although there were many tram conductresses employed by LT, union agreements and the restrictive practices of the era prevented women from driving trams or buses. The bus driving course was projected to last three to four weeks and involved technical training as well as route learning on the new vehicles. The oldest person to be retrained was Albert Jones, aged 66, who would eventually swap his T 7306 motorman badge for a standard N type bus driver's one. Most ex-tram men succeeded in passing the test, but many were reported as wanting to drive their buses in the middle of the road. In truth, old habits died hard.

July opened ominously for the trams, and the feeling of impending doom was heightened when Lord Latham announced that the first stage of tramway abandonment would take place on 1st October. Thereafter, further stages were planned until the final one in October 1952. The whole scheme was to

be known under the rather pathetic code-name of 'Operation Tramaway'. As if to rub in the triumph of the bus brigade, the Tram and Trolleybus Department was merged with Central Buses to form Central Road Services. This really was the beginning of the end as far as the separate identity of the T&T Department was concerned. The scheme also involved the renaming of certain depots – Camberwell became Walworth, Holloway was renamed Highgate, and Streatham, Telford Avenue was dubbed Brixton.

All seemed set for the big switch-over to buses, except that on 11th July, no fewer than 680 permanent way workers gave LT notice of their dissatisfaction. They wanted 10 shillings extra bonus allowance, and vague noises were made about strike action. This might have caused the postponement of stage one of the conversion scheme. However, fears that jobs would be jeopardised were addressed by Lord Latham, who assured everyone that tram drivers and PW workers, who became redundant through conversion, would be found alternative employment within London Transport.

Between 6am on 14th July and 7am on 16th July, a section of the Embankment between Horse Guards Parade and just east of Charing Cross Underground Station was closed to all traffic. This was to facilitate the construction of a Bailey Bridge across the River Thames to the Festival of Britain site on the South Bank. Northbound trams via

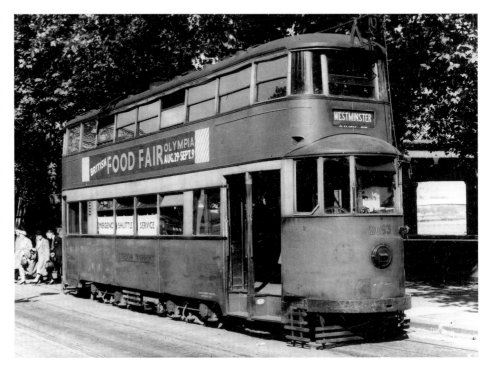

On 20th August 1950, Car 2093 works an emergency shuttle service from Charing Cross to Westminster, whilst a Bailey bridge to the South Bank is put in place. On the adjacent track was Car 2092. J.H.Meredith

Blackfriars Bridge reversed at Savoy Street crossover. However, a few cars continued to Charing Cross and then reversed wrong road back to Savoy Street. The arrangements for trams using the Kingsway Subway were interesting. Southbound cars reversed on the crossover nearest the subway entrance and then ran wrong road on to the Embankment, here they reversed again to proceed towards Blackfriars Bridge. Northbound trams on routes 31, 33 and 35 reversed on the Embankment and entered the subway wrong road, gaining the correct track at the crossover inside the subway entrance. These movements were all controlled by a group of London Transport regulators. In order to reach Blackfriars Bridge northbound 31s were diverted via Lambeth Road and Blackfriars Road, 33s turned right at Lambeth Baths to join cars on service 31. Southbound cars on routes 31 and 33 could not repeat this itinerary as there was no connecting curve between Blackfriars Road and Lambeth Road, therefore they turned left at St George's Circus on to Borough Road. Here cars reversed and proceeded across the Circus to join Lambeth Road. Diverted route 35 trams simply used London Road in both directions. Newspaper reports noted that on Saturday morning hundreds of office cleaners and early workers had to walk part of their journey along the Embankment. On the Westminster side of the obstruction, LT had organised a two car shuttle service from Horse Guards Avenue to the east crossover at Westminster. Each tram kept to its own track. Ex-Walthamstow cars 2058 and 2060 were deployed, each tram bearing a large notice: EMERGENCY SHUTTLE SERVICE.

Eleven days after the first event on Victoria Embankment, London Transport invited the press to a funeral – or, to be more

Left Over the weekend of Saturday 19th August to 6am on Monday 21st August tramway traffic was again interrupted on the Embankment. The 'Westminster Shuttle' was worked by two Feltham cars. This 31 is working temporarily off route due to the Festival of Britain bridge installation. Car 207 is depicted on the Victoria Embankment near Temple Station.

Below John Meredith painstakingly recorded many details of the post-war London tramway scene. He was on hand again at Kennington Road, as Car 184 takes the diversion into Lambeth Road. This set of points was only normally used for emergency purposes, and a 'weekend' pointsman has been employed for the occasion. An LT inspector marches away, seemingly satisfied that all is going according to plan. The date is Sunday 20th August. J.H.Meredith

precise, a cremation. Car 1322 was burnt on 28th July at Penhall Road or Charlton Tramatorium as it was colloquially known. The bonfire was timed and observed by representatives of the London Fire Brigade. It was calculated that almost two trams a day could be disposed of by this method. An escapee from a Penhall Road type farewell was Feltham Car 2097 which arrived in Leeds on 12th August, and emerged from Kirkstall Works on 14th September in the guise of Leeds Car 502.

Meanwhile, although the scrapping programme had commenced, the trams had at least one champion in 66-year-old William Botten, who retired from service at New Cross Depot. He was quoted as saying that trams were the finest form of transport ever devised, and that South London could do with a new fleet and better tracks.

This sentiment was not shared by those directing operations at Penhall Road. Throughout September the tramatorium was made ready. On 6th September, cars 020, 1383, 1385, 1654 and 1762 were noted in the yard. Car 1385 was burnt on the afternoon of 26th September. On the next day, cars 1727, 1744 and accident victim 1396 appeared at Penhall Road. The publicity department had also been active and on 22nd September 'Buses for Trams' notices appeared in the London papers giving details of the first stage of the conversion plan. As the fateful day approached, tram stop signs were removed and replaced by temporary 'dolly' stops, which were then gathered up on the last night of tramway operation. But before the last post was sounded at the end of the month, there were more routine matters to be addressed. Crews of northbound cars on routes 33, 35 and soon to be history route 31, were instructed in case of delay or defect to turn trams at Theobalds Road. Passengers were to be asked to alight at Holborn Station, and told the reason for their curtailed journey. An extra long journey, rather than a curtailed one, was in the minds of a party of German tram enthusiasts who, on 24th September, were treated to a tour of South London. The vehicle used was Car 1988 with Chief Inspector Perry driving and Conductor Downing.

On 29th September, press notices appeared concerning fare rises from 1st October; these seemed to confirm previous suspicions that new buses for old trams wasn't the bargain LT made out. The final day of the Wandsworth and Battersea routes saw many locals taking nostalgic last rides, and by the afternoon trams started leaving Wandsworth Depot for good. All in all, around 70 E/1 cars were removed to Penhall Road. Most came from Clapham and Camberwell depots, and a group of 17 from New

Yet another York Road, this time in Wandsworth, is the setting for the terminus of tram route 12. Car 198 waits its turn to return to Hop Exchange, Borough, whilst an equally doomed 612 trolleybus continues its journey towards Battersea. *N. Rayfield*

Cross were replaced by E/3 cars from Wandsworth and Holloway. Thirty Felthams operating from Brixton were dispatched for temporary store at Charlton before their journey to Leeds. They were replaced by ex-Leyton E/3s from Wandsworth.

Routes 12, 26, 28, 31 and 34 faded from existence to be replaced by RT type diesel buses, as was trolleybus route 612. An interesting quirk of route 34 was that it was the only post-war service to pass two change pits, in Gresham Road and Coldharbour Lane. All the other routes withdrawn at this stage worked solely over the conduit. The 34 also achieved some celebrity by the number of changes of direction as it wended its way from Blackfriars to the short lived terminus at Battersea Bridge. A pleasant aspect to this route was the ride on Long Lane by Clapham Common and down the hill at Cedars Road. Another feature of note on routes 12 and 31 was the existence of railway level crossings on Nine Elms Lane. The section of track along Southwark Street traversed by route 26 was not abandoned at this stage, but was given over to route 72 cars which now terminated at Hop Exchange.

Some idea of the atmosphere on the last night can be gathered from this contemporary newspaper report:

It was pouring with rain, dark and gloomy, when we started off from Battersea Bridge at 11.55pm on Saturday night. At the Latchmere, somebody asked: 'This is the last tram, mate?' 'Yes,' the conductor replied wearily. In they came, about half a dozen people. The conductor moved forward for his fares, fingering his ticket rack. It was only then that we really took any notice of the two police cars that had been travelling behind us during our journey. By that time the lower deck was full. Then it was noticed that when the passengers received their tickets, instead of crumpling them up in the usual way, they carefully put them in their inside coat pockets. 'One of the last 34 tickets – I'm keeping it as a souvenir.' – one passenger confided to me as he showed his penny ha'penny ticket.

A supporter of the Light Railway Transport League sat gloomily in the corner. 'A tram lover' – observed the conductor.

All along the route people stood in groups at the tram stops. Some waved, a lot laughed, none cried. Past Crash Corner (ruins of Hemmings Bakers) we went, up Cedars Road, responsible for many tram accidents on the 34 route, and so to Clapham. A knot of small boys, notebooks in hand, eagerly watched our approach, and as we drew alongside, jotted our number down. 'More tram spotters' – somebody remarked.

Above In Nine Elms Lane route 12 cars had to traverse a number of railway sidings leading from Nine Elms Goods Depot to wharves on the Thames. Railway wagons were normally shunted across the road by a vehicle similar to a farmer's tractor.
D.A.Thompson

Below Car 1573 turns from Blackfriars Road into Southwark Street. Behind the tram is Blackfriars Bridge, and on the right of the picture is the embankment carrying railway lines to Blackfriars and Holborn Viaduct stations. The section of track in Southwark Street saw further service when route 72 trams were extended to Hop Exchange in place of the axed routes 12 and 26.
D.A.Thompson

One solitary passenger remained by the time we reached Brixton – and then it happened. A crowd of people headed by two white jacketed waiters, a photographer and a policeman rushed towards us from a brilliantly lit café. Our driver, Robert E. Kenna, four years with London Transport, stopped the tram and his cabin was instantly besieged by the crowd. The waiters handed something to the driver – it was a large glistening bottle of whisky! 'We often drop in there for a cup of tea, but we never expected anything like this' – enthused conductor Frederick Lawrence, who has been eighteen months with London Transport . . .

Then we arrived at the depot. Row upon row of trams, like so many empty boxes, bleak and still. An official looked at them 'I'm sorry to see them go' he mused, 'we have had plenty of trouble with them, but they've been good old friends.' – Thus the 34 was no more.

Car 195 was the last tram to leave Wandsworth on route 31. After its departure in the early hours of Sunday, 1st October, the crowd gradually drifted away. The last route 12 car from Hop Exchange to Wandsworth was recorded as E/3 Car 1959. In the morning a different set of transport devotees would be out with their cameras trained on the new RT buses operating routes 44, 45,

168, 169 and 170. The tram supporters could take a crumb of comfort from the sight on Monday morning of a route 72 car at Hop Exchange, but it was poor recompense for the sad events of stage one of the conversion scheme.

On 1st October a total of 58 'new' cars was noted in Penhall Road Yard. They were all E/1s, both standard and reconditioned, from New Cross, Camberwell and Wandsworth depots. The next day, E/1 Car 1656 was torched by the scrappers. Some 20 Felthams were also spotted awaiting transport to Leeds, and by 21st October, six had departed for the North. On 29th October, only 26 of the 58 cars delivered to Penhall Road at the beginning of the month, remained to face their fate.

Whilst the enthusiasts picked over the minutiae of the night before, most other Londoners found of more immediate interest the revision of fares applicable from 1st October. In general, fare rises look moderate by modern standards; for instance ticket values below 7d went up by a halfpenny, and in the range from 7d to 1s 2d, by a penny. The real blow fell on transfer, workmen's and return fares, which were abolished. Basically, LT had inherited a complex fare structure from the LCC and the other municipal and

Above Clapham Junction terminus was situated in St John's Hill. Tram routes 26 and 28 originally ran to Hammersmith and Harlesden respectively, but these useful through services had been severed by the pre-war trolleybus conversion programme – hence this rather unnatural end to the tracks.

Below The wide waterfront vista of the Thames at Lambeth is the background to car 1945 as it turns from the Albert Embankment into Lambeth Road. Just behind the tram is the entrance to Lambeth Bridge, which in its rebuilt state (it was reopened by King George V on 19th July 1932), was designed to take double tram tracks. However, well-to-do factions on the other side of the River soon put paid to any plans the LCC had to run trams in exclusive Westminster! D.A.Thompson

company tramways. This produced some odd quirks, such as the fact that Croydon seemed to retain its own 'independent' fare table, whereby on services 16 and 18 it was sometimes more economic to rebook at the Norbury Boundary. The transfer possibilities, especially of the 7d single and 11d return – and corresponding 4d midday cheap fare – were extensive. Returns did not even require the passenger to go back to his starting point. Indeed, if they were punched for Transfer A or B, the conductor had no means of telling. The last link with the 'old regime' was severed when crews were instructed not to use the word WORKMAN on the destination blinds.

Of course, the imminent removal of the

trams stirred many borough councils into action and the expense of road improvements concentrated the minds of local town hall staff. In Lewisham proposals were published for rebuilding the Clock Tower area. The principal aim was to stop traffic jams and to provide for a projected increase in bus numbers after the trams had been replaced. Nearer to the centre of town, the perennial problem of what to do with the Kingsway Subway also surfaced. London Transport were quoted as saying that two years work would be necessary to widen the subway to take two streams of traffic. Adequate ventilation would also be vital, as would be a lessening of the exit gradient in Holborn.

The second great talking point in late

spring 1950 revolved around the reinstatement of the carriageway after tramlines had been removed. Local authorities suddenly began to get the wind up when it was revealed that, according to the letter of the law, roads had to be left as they were when the tram tracks were laid. Councils would then have to discover what road surfaces existed before the trams, so that financial accounts with London Transport could be settled. Of course, in view of increased traffic, the idea of leaving, for example, the Old Kent Road in the same condition as it was in 1870, was nonsensical. What was also noticed by councillors was the fact that, when the trams went and the track was lifted, the rating income on the permanent way would be lost. Instead LT would pay bus licence duty straight to the national exchequer. As the South London boroughs flapped, London Transport suddenly showed a not so unexpected coyness about highway reinstatement, and there the matter rested for a while.

Top On 12th September 1937, trolleybus route 612 was inaugurated using the turning loop into Candahar Road. On 6th June 1949, the date of this photograph, any thoughts of further trolleybus extensions had evaporated in face of the official enthusiasm for diesel buses. Car 1781 is in Battersea Park Road by the entrance to Candahar Road. J.H.Meredith

Left The motorman of Car 1381 checks oncoming traffic one more time before he proceeds round the corner into Clapham Common North Side. Also at the corner of the street is a fine example of an original LCC clover leaf stop sign. In the distance Cedars Road drops down to meet Lavender Hill at the fateful intersection by the baker's shop. D.A.Thompson

Whilst some had track removal on their minds, others could rejoice on 11th June to see the northern half of the new County Hall roundabout open to trams and other traffic. At approximately 9.40am that Sunday, HR/2 Car 1877 traversed the new track in York Road and Addington Street. Car 1877 also tried out the new terminal stub in Addington Street. According to the *London Transport Magazine* of May 1950, the consulting engineer for the new County Hall roundabout was Robert Macintyre, Permanent Way Engineer (Trams). This was to be Mr Macintyre's last job before retiring. His career with the former LCC Tramways began in 1910. Later in the year, on 22nd October, at eight o'clock in the morning, the southern half of the County Hall roundabout was opened to trams. This was for through cars working from Westminster Bridge Road on to Westminster Bridge; the curves leading into Lambeth Palace Road, used only by routes 22 and 24, had to wait until the afternoon for the first test car. As this new track was commissioned, so local contractors got to work in the Wandsworth/Battersea areas on rail removal. As an interim measure tramlines were filled with an asphalt mixture, but the conduit slot was left visible. Depending on the work load, a gang would arrive days or sometimes weeks later to cordon off one side of the carriageway so that either the up or the down track could be lifted. Many frontagers complained about the noise of pneumatic drills as they sliced into large chunks of the road surface. Granite setts were normally lifted with the old surface, but at certain locations track, conduit and setts were all buried under a new asphalt layer. Rails were generally cut up on site and then carted away by lorry to be sold as scrap metal. Pointwork which contained large amounts of recoverable steel was particularly valuable. Wood blocks were sold as logs for open fires. Well tarred, they burnt well! Wandsworth Borough Council was quoted as needing to spend £428,000 on removing 11½ miles (18.4 km) of track and reinstating the carriageway.

The trams carried their usual seasonal shopping traffic as Christmas approached. There had been some misgivings about implementation of stage one of the conversion programme, but the press and London Transport were already focussed on the second stage which would take place early in January. As if to emphasise the unstoppable nature of the enterprise, just before the festive season tram stop signs started to be removed from the Wimbledon, Tooting, and Clapham areas. The process of abandonment had acquired a lethal momentum, and 1951 would see a substantial proportion of the remaining system swept away.

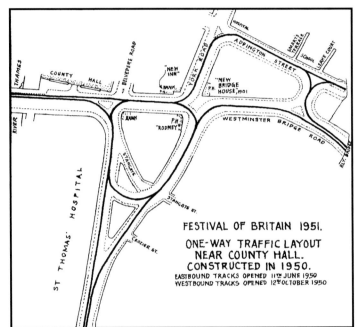

FESTIVAL OF BRITAIN 1951.
ONE-WAY TRAFFIC LAYOUT
NEAR COUNTY HALL.
CONSTRUCTED IN 1950.
EASTBOUND TRACKS OPENED 11TH JUNE 1950
WESTBOUND TRACKS OPENED 12TH OCTOBER 1950

Above Long Road bisects Clapham Common and offered on Car 593 a pleasant tree lined ride, a world away from the hustle and bustle of some other South London streets. D.A. Thompson

Below At Hop Exchange, Borough, Car 2046 has taken possession of the terminus after routes 12 and 26 quit the scene. Tramlines at this location should have been connected with those in Tooley Street, but the status quo was maintained and through services were never routed past London Bridge Station. J.H. Meredith

We begin this chapter with one of the author's favourite photographs. The motorman prepares to board Car 1941 just as his conductor steps out with the tea can. Both crew members will no doubt share a cup of Rosy Lee *en route* as traffic conditions permit. W.J.Wyse

LIFE ON THE TRAMS

AFTER THE exertions and turmoil of the Second World War, London Transport found that a loyal staff was its greatest asset. Consequently, the sometimes harsh working conditions and petty disciplines of the inter-war years were toned down or phased out altogether. Right up to the 1930s the management and many inspectors were regarded with fear or loathing; sometimes an inspector would command respect for his fair and impartial behaviour, but the threat of losing one's job for a comparatively minor misdemeanour was still a very real one. In pre-war days one was expected to drive an open fronted tramcar for up to nine hours without a break. Refreshments, such as they were, had to be consumed 'on the road', and wives and children of motormen and conductors could be seen going out to the trams of their loved ones to hand over a hot tea can or a bite to eat. Also, crews were expected to work anywhere on the old LCC system. How

you got from, say, Holloway late shift one day, to New Cross early shift next day, was your own problem!

In the period covered by this book, conditions had improved. The community of tramway workers was a close-knit one, and in many respects the discipline which many men had experienced in military service was carried over into everyday life. The working week had been reduced to 44 hours, no single duty exceeded 8 hours, and each shift had to include a 40-minute meal break. In 1948 a tram conductor could earn £5 15s a week (in 1952 tramway workers achieved parity with LT Central Bus rates, and drivers received £7 4s 6d per week, whilst conductors earned the sum of £7 2s 6d) and if an experienced conductor took out a trainee to show him the ropes, he received two shillings extra for the shift. 'Spreadover duties' which could be three to four hours morning peak followed by time off then another couple of

hours in the evening peak, were now properly funded, and Saturday afternoon and Sunday duties were paid at an increased rate. The working week ran from Sunday to Saturday, alternating between early and late shifts. Every seven weeks a crew member would have two consecutive rest days; on the other weeks he was entitled to a day off which advanced with each week, i.e. Monday one week, Tuesday the next week, and so on.

How the £5 15s fitted in with the standard of living can be gauged by a few contemporary prices: a bar of Palmolive soap cost 5d, a pair of shoes for a gentleman £1 6s, a lady's winter coat £2 15s, and for those with a sweet tooth a Mars bar could be had for 3d. A real treat for the LTE higher-ups would be a return air trip to watch their sportsmen and women compete against teams representing the Paris Metro. The return, London to Paris, cost £15. The social

Beneath hanging baskets of flowers a pointsman plies his trade. There was only one set of automatic conduit points, at the junction of Denmark Hill and Coldharbour Lane. All the rest had to be changed the old fashioned way.
J.C.Gillham

TRACK UP

THE delayed replacement of existing tram services by buses has thrown a heavy burden on the tram permanent way division. Track gangs, seriously weakened since the end of the war by retirements, face a heavy maintenance programme.

To fill the gaps in the ranks of the skilled men a training school has been started at Rye Lane depot. Men from the gangs were asked to offer themselves for training, and the first class of twelve began last November. To fill their places in the gangs labourers were recruited. Each class trains in the school for two weeks ; then it goes out on the road as a training gang under its instructor to gain experience in actual repair work. As the men pass a proficiency test they are posted to permanent gangs.

The mass of steel work which lies under the roads. In the school the class is taught how to assemble and dismantle a section of conduit track. Left to right : F. Ednett, instructor A. Barker, H. Smart, ganger J. Turton, A. Dye and T. Green.

Selected men are trained in electric arc welding, oxy-acetylene cutting or rail grinding. Sixty-seven-year-old Arthur Pugh (left) watches his pupil Frank Davies welding a track crossing. Right, depot foreman C. Earwaker.

After two weeks at Rye Lane depot trainees get practical experience outside. Supervising work is 62-year-old instructor A. Barker (centre). Forty years on permanent way work, he helped lay the first conduit track in London.

Tom Websell, training as a checkburner in the school, learns to cut quickly and accurately through a rail with an oxy-acetylene flame. Right, George Bennett—25 years a checkburner.

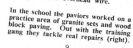

An important job is grinding down steel deposited on the track by welding. Above, you see the machine used for this at work—it is powered from the current rail or overhead wire.

In the school the paviors worked on a practice area of granite sets and wood block paving. Out with the training gang they tackle real repairs (right).

9

and sports side was particularly developed in the organisation and the Tram & Trolleybus department football team, which at one time drew no fewer than three members from the Charlton Works staff, won several national competitions in the late 1940s and early 1950s.

If fitness was not an employee's strong point, or if a crew member became sick or infirm, he would be transferred to lighter duties such as pointsman or plough shifter at a conduit change pit. Whether this *was* a lighter duty was debatable, but at least during the last years of London's trams, most pointsmen were supplied with a canvas hut to keep out the worst of the elements. Auto-

Right This is how to do it – you pull the point iron and lean back. Charlton staff Car 330 has just been directed on to the entrance track to home base. Waiting for the right of way is works Car 012.

Drivers crossing Tooting Broadway had to be pretty adept at power and coast techniques, since there were numerous dead sections of conduit lying in wait for the unwary. On 21st August 1949, Car 1492 seems to be over the worst and is pulling away along Mitcham Road. The bus is standing on the fossilised, abandoned northbound curve from Tooting High Street. A.B. Cross

matic 'power or coast' points were installed on Denmark Hill at the junction with Coldharbour Lane, where routes 34 and 48 diverged from the Dog Kennel Hill services. On the overhead wire section they could be found at Well Hall Circus and the Yorkshire Grey Roundabout. Pointsmen were employed during the day at most conduit equipped junctions; after they went off duty motormen were expected in time honoured fashion to descend from their trams and place the point iron in a hatchway in the road. Longevity at work seemed to be common amongst pointsmen; *London Transport Magazine* for November 1948 carried a couple of paragraphs on the retirement of 71-year-old George Hubbard, who had put in 50 years service on the tramways. Mr Hubbard was well known to crews as for fourteen years he had been controlling tramway movements at Tooting Broadway. This was a particularly difficult junction to oversee – not only did the points need to be set correctly, but a motorman of a tram going from Streatham to Clapham had to negotiate no fewer than 10 breaks in the current supply.

If his attention wandered or another road vehicle stopped suddenly in front of him, then the car would be 'stuck on a dead' until the following tram arrived to nudge it forward. Another tribute was paid in the April 1950 issue, when Tom Phillips, also with 50 years service, retired from his job pulling the point lever at Camberwell Green.

One of the perks of the job was the entitlement to free travel. All tram personnel were issued with a pass and this saved on off duty expenses. This pass earned the nickname of a 'sticky', and although it was not issued to spouses, when couples went out shopping by tram or on a visit with the family, most conductors turned a blind eye to this particular form of extended misuse. However, there was another side of the coin where old disciplinary practices died hard. If a conductor turned up late for a duty he was sent home without pay for that day. This loss of income was the cause of some bad feeling amongst LT employees, and the situation

Although women had been employed in London during both world wars as bus and tram conductresses, they had never been allowed to drive trams. In this respect London lagged behind Glasgow which had a number of all female tram crews. From a modern point of view, some 1950s employment laws appear more in tune with Victorian thinking, and they certainly discriminated against large sections of society. On what seems to be a last day lark, two ladies hijack the controls of LRTL special car 1908 in an attempt to get away from Addington Street one way system.

was compounded by the fact that there was also no sick pay to cover genuine illness – nor was there any provision for a pension scheme.

Potential recruits to the tramway department could apply first to one of the divisional offices: Manor House for North London, Vauxhall for the South West and Camberwell for the South East. A selection test and a medical followed, after which a period of practical training in the art of being a conductor or a motorman was necessary. Conductors were then placed with a more experienced crew member and they survived in a sink or swim manner.

Drivers were sent to the Clapham Motor School, where they received expert instruction on a variety of disciplines connected with tram driving. It was expected that every motorman had knowledge of his vehicle and the current supply system so that he could effect minor running repairs as the need arose. In charge of the Clapham setup was Chief Instructor E. E. Wallis, ably assisted by Instructors E. Hancock, C. Holman and A. Sharman. Stan Collins was also one of the team and his memoirs, published in 1977 under the title of *The Wheels Used To Talk To Us* (Sheaf Publishing), give one of the most detailed pictures of the London tramway scene.

Each trainee had both theory and practice sessions, where the function of the controller, the magnetic brakes and the hand brake were explained. A life size section of conduit complete with plough served as an instruction model. Another model was built to a scale of one inch to five feet (1:60) and was a replica of the Elephant and Castle road junction. It was constructed by Acting

Regulator C. Thorpe and Driver A. H. Sharman, son of the Instructor. Drivers were shown the complexities of the six way tram junction in miniature, together with the position of the fourteen sets of traffic lights.

Road practice was under the careful eye of a senior inspector; normally a standard E/1 would be used. Although the familiar red and white L plates were not compulsory on trams, nevertheless they were made an appearance. Indicator blinds were turned to SPECIAL. This word could also be applied to Mr Wallis's favourite tests, whereby on a slight downgrade, he would stand on the back platform, put the controller into reverse and cut out the magnetic braking. The motorman would then be given the bell to stop the car, and finding he had no magnetic brakes, he had to rely on the hand brake to bring the tram to a halt. This was the theory! If the rooky motorman lost his composure, Chief Instructor Wallis was on hand at the rear platform to replace the controller key. Candidates who failed first time were normally given extra coaching by Messrs Collins and Sharman.

After successfully satisfying LT requirements, the new motorman was passed out to his depot. Here he might spend a couple of days learning the routes. In the case of New Cross Depot which supplied cars for a number of different services, this process took somewhat longer. An exception to this rule was Holloway Depot where all tram drivers had to have at least six months experience on other routes before being allowed through the Kingsway Subway. This rule became a problem at Holloway after 1940, when it was left operating only the Kingsway Subway routes and therefore had to import new recruits from South London depots. The difficulty of persuading staff to transfer became so acute in 1949 that on 10th November two runnings on each of routes 31 and 33 were moved out to Wandsworth and Norwood respectively. As newly qualified drivers could not work spare turns, ex-motormen who were now trolleybus drivers had to cover for absent colleagues. Tramway staff could be expected to work different routes on one shift, unlike their more pampered central bus counterparts. A Holloway duty, for

example, might consist of a complete round trip on service 35 followed by a similar turn on route 33. These return journeys were referred to as 'rounders', and the Kingsway Subway was known to crews as the 'tunnel' – trams on routes 31, 33 and 35 were 'tunnel cars'.

After initial training, staff went on the spare list where they were required to cover any vacant duty caused by absence of a regular crew member; a year was sometimes spent on the spare roster. When booking on for a duty, the conductor would be supplied with his ticket box which had a duty number and a route allocation. The conductor would then consult a board to see his tram and the motorman allocated to that tram. The two crew members would then make their charge fit for the road, and if they were on one of the Embankment 'circles' they had to face the prospect of no 'stand time' in central London, therefore refreshments en route were a necessity. Crews normally relied on a can of hot tea or coffee to see them through; this could always be replenished at certain spots on route. For example, a crew working routes 36/38 (Abbey Wood to Embankment) could use the following authorised (by LT) refreshment places: 176 Woolwich Church Street, 501 Woolwich Road, Eatwell Café in Woolwich Church Street, and Dunbar's Café at 725 Old Kent Road. Of course all this

liquid refreshment had a natural effect on staff. Fr Benedict Sankey can recall being a passenger on a route 40 car which sailed along Camberwell New Road in full parallel until Kennington was reached. The motorman then put on the 'anchors' (brakes) and disappeared down some stairs at a strategically placed public convenience. These facilities were sometimes placed in the middle or alongside tram tracks, and existed at most important junctions and termini such as Elephant and Castle, Bricklayers Arms and Beresford Square.

The life of a post-war motorman can perhaps be best illustrated by the following account written by Roy Hubble. The full text, which has been edited here, was published in the *Tramway and Light Railway Society Bulletin* for Spring/Summer 1966. Roy lived in Catford and from 1949 his interest in trams had developed into a serious study. He had become acquainted with Rob, a driver from New Cross Depot:

One fine evening Rob and I boarded a 54 tram at Catford en route for New Cross. With a curt 'He's with me' to the conductor, Rob climbed up the stairs hotly pursued by his 15-year-old companion. We sat, as you may guess, in the front bay, sometimes looking out at the road ahead, but occasionally looking down the interior of the car observing the floating of the bodywork as the car sped on

Time for a chat! At Rainton Road crossover, Charlton, the driver of Car 1503 leans out to pass a few comments to his opposite number on Car 1656. Whether the conversation was about the dent in Car 1503's dash, we shall never know. It is more likely that the 40 was running late and has transferred its passengers to the following car before reversing to go back to town. J.H.Meredith

All hands to the pumps at Abbey Wood, as staff and inspectors try to remedy a problem with the trolley pole. We can assume the bunch of flowers crossing the road is not in the safe keeping of the man with the trolley rope! At any rate the chap on the outside of the top deck has a grandstand view of the proceedings, and is obviously directing operations for his ground crew.
R.Hubble

its journey to the depot. 'These E/1s might be old,' I thought, 'but they can still go.' Reaching the depot, we walked up the incline and on to the traverser. One fitter objected, but Rob spoke to him rather sharply, and all was well. The depot itself was very interesting, there being a number of out of service cars parked at the back, awaiting repair as a result of breakdowns or collisions (New Cross had its fair share of both).

After speaking to a friendly electrician, we walked towards a car standing on its own, which was scheduled to go out on service in a short time. It was one of the 1930 E/1 cars. These had new bodies when built, but the trucks and equipments came from the old single deck Kingsway Subway cars. We boarded the car and Rob showed me how a driver should check over a car before he drives it from the depot. We did everything: bells, lights, lifeguards, controllers, brakes, sand gear and so on. Rob then showed me how to apply the handbrake correctly. It was turned in a clockwise direction, using the ratchet when the handle became difficult to turn as the brakes tightened up. The correct way to release this brake was to release the ratchet and keep hold of the handle as it unwound, at the same time applying a notch of power, which would result in a smooth start. If the brake was fully unwound before power was applied, there would be an uncomfortable jerk as the car started.

Next came the most interesting part, namely, the controller. Rob showed me the correct manner of operation by placing his hand over mine on the handle, and then going through the motions of notching up, switching off and braking. Of course, the car was stationary all this time with the circuit breakers switched out. Most London controllers had eight power notches and seven brake notches. To start, the controller was turned in a clockwise direction, pausing at each notch just long enough to feel the increase in speed before advancing to the next notch. On the first four notches the motors were connected in series. There was a gap followed by a further four notches, but the motors were now connected in parallel. One point to remember was if the power was to be kept on for some time, the handle should only be placed in either the fourth or the eighth notch. The other notches were for acceleration purposes only, and the use of these for normal running would in time burn out the resistances. It sometimes happened, that in thick traffic or fog, drivers would, instead of notching up quickly, switching off and coasting, run on the first one or two notches. The result of this was that the resistances, which in London cars were situated under the platforms, would get hot enough to set the platform boards on fire. This, to the passengers, could be somewhat frightening!

Rob explained that the controller handle must never be notched back, but should be smartly brought back to the off position. Failure to carry this out would cause excessive arcing and would burn out the controller contacts.

The operation of the brake was much the same as notching up, pausing at each notch long enough to feel the braking effect. However, Rob emphasised that with electric braking one point must be remembered: the faster the car was travelling, the greater the available braking power. This was because the car's motors were converted into generators for braking. If a tram was travelling between 25 and 30 mph (40–50 kmh), a braking effect would be noticeable on the first brake notch, but at half this speed, the first two or three notches would be ineffective.

Additionally, this electro-magnetic brake would only slow down and stop the car, but would not hold it at a stop – the hand brake had to be used for this purpose.

It can be appreciated that driving a London tram at walking pace in heavy traffic called for some judgement with regard to efficient braking. It is not surprising that there were a number of slow speed collisions which, if air brakes had been universally adopted, would have been avoided.

Another instruction which Rob gave me at this time was that the controller must always be placed in the off position when negotiating section gaps. These gaps in supply occurred every half mile or so. Overhead routes were quite simple in this respect, but the conduit routes were more awkward. If a car went over a gap with power on, particularly at slow speed, there was a severe jolt as the car lost then regained power, accompanied by an unhealthy flash from the collector gear – trolley or plough. On the conduit system there were additional gaps at all pointwork which robbed the car of power when it was most needed. This is why London trams approached junctions at speed, with the driver constantly switching on and off power. Even a good driver (and there were few at New Cross in the post-war years) could sometimes get stuck on a 'dead' and have to be pushed off by a following car.

A too violent application of the brake would cause the tram to skid and form flats on the wheels with a noticeable result.

Roy then continues to describe several trips he made under Rob's guidance, one of which resulted in his driving a tram past the family home in Bromley Road, Catford. He notes with some satisfaction that he rang the tram gong just to let the folks know that he was passing! Roy further describes some individual cars.

Car 1570 was a good car; it ran well and was very quiet, which was unusual for E/1s or any London car for that matter. The noisiest trams in London were the ex-Walthamstow cars, closely followed by the E/1s fitted with Metropolitan Vickers equipment The E/3s had a high pitched whine which made the cars sound as if they were going much faster than they really were. The HR/2 cars had a very distinctive gear sound unlike any others, and could always be recognised, even at great distances. Passengers waiting at a stop in Catford would always look at me in disbelief when I would announce that the tram approaching in the distance would be a 58, a route always worked by HR/2 cars.

Car 1570 remained a very quiet car until overhauled at Charlton some time in 1950. She emerged from the works fully repainted; noticeable were the red painted axle box springs on the trucks, and after this overhaul

You can't keep a good man down – this fellow certainly takes risks for his employers (in those days health and safety laws were rather rudimentary). Here at Beresford Square the trolley pole *voodoo* seems to have struck again, and a line of cars is starting to build up along Plumstead Road. For the technically minded, the overhead wire going off to left into Woolwich New Road is supported by double pull off hangers, whilst the wire over the stricken tramcar has single trolleybus style hangers. R.Hubble

she sounded like any other E/1 in the fleet. This tram was finally withdrawn in January 1951. It was fitted with English Electric controllers.

After a few trips on the 74 it was time for Rob's meal break. Our next car, still on route 74, was E/1 rehab 1190. Although rebuilt, this car retained its original Westinghouse equipment, and Rob did not like it very much, as it suffered from 'tight blocks' – in other words, the hand brake was badly adjusted. A big disadvantage with Westinghouse controllers was that, in order to cut out a motor, the controller cover had to be removed and adjustments made to the contact fingers. On other controllers a motor could be cut out by using the reversing key to turn a knob either on the top or at the back of the controller, obviating the necessity to remove the cover. Westinghouse equipment as

a rule meant a slow car, and this was also not appreciated by Rob. Routes 68 and 70 were worked from New Cross Depot using slow cars, usually the 1930 E/1 type. These routes were always referred to by the crews as the 'slow road'.

Rob was quite a character; on a cold day when a tram's platform was not the warmest of places, he would quite happily wear an ex-RAF fur-lined jacket and flying boots. He had some frightening habits: he would leave the controller on, and while the car was at speed, make an adjustment to the headlamp (from the outside). Another of these habits was to lean out of the entrance, again with power on and at speed, to get a good look at the indicator of a tram going in the opposite direction. One night I was standing in Catford with a group of friends, when we heard the high pitched whine of a tram speeding down Bromley Road. It was ME/3 Car 1370. It had not had to stop at the request stop at

A view from the stairs to the controller of an E/3 car gives us some idea of the platform layout of a London tramcar of the post-war era. D.A.Thompson

Canadian Avenue, and so by the time it approached us, it was doing a good 30 mph and in true E/1 tradition was rocking and swaying in all directions. As can be guessed, the driver was Rob, and on seeing me, he leaned out and gave a sporting gesture as he went past. He returned to the job in hand, and we observed the car fly round the curve, almost on its side, and heard the groan of the magnetic track brake fully applied as the car stopped at St Lawrence's Church. Although he taught me to drive correctly, Rob was the first to admit that he was the world's worst driver himself. He said he did not particularly like trams and was eager to transfer to buses.

In January 1952, I boarded E/3 Car 1927 at Catford Town Hall. The conductor was a stranger to me, but the driver was very familiar, I sat on the top deck and was there for a few minutes, when the conductor came and spoke to me. 'Excuse me sir, the driver would like to speak to you at the front.' I went down the stairs and had a chat with Rob. During the course of our conversation he calmly went into the lower saloon and removed the fare table, which he gave to me, saying: 'There is only three days to go, so I don't think they will miss this.' As we climbed Downham Way, Rob handed the controls to me and I took the car to Grove Park terminus. Although it was broad daylight, nobody seemed to take any notice. I was taller now and was also wearing Rob's hat.

E/3 Car 1927 was one of a large number newer cars transferred to New Cross Depot from other depots as the South London conversion proceeded. However, I shared Rob's opinion that many of these cars were not as good as some of the E/1 cars which had already been scrapped. The E/3s were slower and harder riding than some of the E/1s, and also the brakes were very sharp. From the passengers' point of view they were an improvement, particularly the top deck seating, which was fully upholstered, unlike the standard E/1s. Personally, I had always liked the appearance of the E/3s, particularly those which retained their original aluminium drivers' screens. From the mid-thirties onwards, spare parts for these Alpax screens were no longer purchased, and from then on any car involved in a serious collision had its original screen replaced by a Charlton wooden one. A high dash was frequently fitted, but occasionally the difference in height was made up by the addition of a sheet of metal or canvas attached to the bottom of the screen. These original metal screens had only one real disadvantage, there was a joint above the driver's head which incorporated a cork liner and was hardly noticeable when it was painted. However, when the cork was perished, this joint would let in water rather badly. I remember seeing car 1924 with the top of both its screens painted with black waterproof paint to prevent leaking. This was unusual, as the easiest temporary cure was to place a sandbag on top of the screen to cover the bad joint.

I have seen sandbags used for other purposes, the most common example was the use of a sandbag at the top of the stairs on E/1 cars to prevent the bulkhead door from flying open. The floating of the bodywork would sometimes lift the door catch out of alignment, allowing the door to fly open and letting an uncomfortable draught blow on the back of the driver's neck.

With the possible exception of Car 1, and a few MET cars, no London tram was fitted with windscreen wipers. There were two small windows in the front screen, which could be opened downwards, allowing the driver to wipe the glass and then close it again in wet weather. He could of course run with the window down, which somewhat defeated the object of having a windscreen in the first place. Rob showed me a windscreen wiper made out of an old wooden clothes peg; most drivers had these, and in wet weather fitted them on to one of the small windows, working them to and fro to clean the glass as required. Another piece of unofficial equipment was a match box which was used to wedge the driving mirror in the open position.

I arranged to meet Rob on his last night as a tram driver. I met his car at Catford and was pleased to see it was HR/2 Car 1857. Unfortunately, however, I never had the chance to drive it. Car 1857 had a faulty hand brake and Rob was having great difficulty in holding the car at stops on Downham Way. He said he was fed up with it and was running it in on the next trip. [Defective trams were usually taken back to their home depot, where the driver had to report to a depot official for further instructions. At the end of the shift the driver had to fill out a defects card – author.] When the HR/2 cars were transferred to New Cross from Camberwell, the depot staff had disconnected the slipper brake mechanism and, from then onwards, the hand brakes always gave trouble. I alighted from the car at Catford and wished Rob good luck with bus driving.

The study of overhead wiring forms a fascinating science by itself. On Eltham Road, Lee, the emergency wagon has been summoned to fix a break in the trolley wire and to clamp the running wire carrying the traction current back into the ear. The ear clamp was then bolted to the hanger on the span wire. D.Mackenzie

Sometimes snowbrooms didn't appear where they were most needed. It doesn't look like one has reached Well Hall Road, Eltham, and the tram men are having to clear the track themselves in the face of deteriorating weather conditions. Out of shot of the photograph on the right hand side of the street, in front of St John's Church, was an LCC shelter for tramway workers. Its telephone numbers – OT 126 and 654 – were listed in the official (i.e. not available to the public) timetable, and one can assume that a call has been made to New Cross Depot to request the relevant mechanical assistance. R.Hubble

Although Roy omits to mention it in his account, in conversation with the author he did point out that during foggy weather both front and rear fog lights were switched on; these lights were not fitted to ex-East Ham and West Ham cars until 1947.

Whilst the mechanics of tram driving fascinated Roy, the art of overhead wiring was of particular interest to Father Benedict Sankey. He adds his own comments on a hitherto neglected area of study:

On my second visit to the Thornton Heath branch I noticed that the bracket poles had been stripped of their scrollwork, and the bowstrings and associated hangers had been replaced by trolleybus style hangers and spacer bars – all rather ugly, I thought. The Wimbledon line, ex-LUT, was different; up to 1946 it had retained its LUT insulated bolt hangers and pull offs, which were replaced by LCC style non insulated fittings. The use of trolleybus fittings was not confined to Thornton Heath and its bracket poles. The same was done on the two centre poles that survived in Croydon; where two wires were close together at Grove Park terminus (a legacy of the bow and pantograph trials?); on the northern approach to Well Hall Round-about; and outside Brixton Hill Depot. Single trolleybus style hangers were employed at Wimbledon terminus, where they were presumably installed when the trolleybus loop was put in.

The line through Woolwich and on to Abbey Wood was distinguished by the sharing of the trolleybus positive wire as far as Bostall Hill, where the wider roads allowed a separate tram wire. At Abbey Wood terminus and other corners, where the tram wire needed to follow its own alignment, single trolleybus style hangers were employed. I remember reading that in preparation for through running, Croydon had to give up their 'open skyline' bracket arm construction and change to span wires and central running. Then they bought trams with two trolleys which were necessarily out of centre! On single track sections the wires were widely spaced, so that on the 33s and 78s you would see an E/3 running with the wire in line with the trolley that was not in use.

Breakdown Tender 173K has been called out on 2nd April 1951 to aid Car 1493 which has broken its plough carrier at the trailing points in the foreground. The use of Addington Street siding for disabled trams was a not infrequent occurrence. J.H.Meredith

The facing points at the entry to the roundabouts at either end of Westhorne Avenue were the last example of the LCC's automatic points technique. A skate in the overhead was set well back from the junction (where the driver would be less concerned with what the other traffic was doing and could do his power/coast selection undistracted). The skate controlled a frog which split the overhead line, and the trolley wheel then encountered a plain contactor which operated the appropriate point coil. On the postwar system this also occurred at Herne Hill junction (routes 33, 78 and 48).

Another witness to the daily routine of tramway workers, Gerald Druce, has recorded individual behaviour from crews at change pits. On his daily journeys to and from school Gerald Druce noted the following antics:

Streatham Change Pit was at the bottom of the hill from the junction of the Croydon and Tooting lines at St Leonard's Church, then the cars had to climb up the railway overbridge at Streatham Station. Officially, southbound cars had to stop just before the pit, whilst the conductor alighted to release

the pole from its hook and put it on the wire. One Thornton Heath crew, with whom I travelled several times, were distinguished by their ability to go through the change pit non stop.

Down the hill the conductor rode on the rear bumper, unwinding the rope from the cleat and, as there was sufficient overlap of conduit and overhead, released the pole from its hook, and with unerring aim guided the trolley wheel on to the overhead. Meanwhile, the driver had reduced speed to some 10 mph (16 kmh) and locked the controller at 'off' to release the key which he used to operate the changeover switch under the staircase. By the time he turned round again and had released the controller, the conductor signalled success with two rings on the bell, and the tram continued up the hill. – All this sort of conduct was of course frowned on by the powers that be, and at only one other change pit, Lee Green (eastbound), could trams (legally) shoot their ploughs at speed.

The motorman responsible for the 'through running' at Streatham was subsequently identified as Driver R. R. Randall of Thornton Heath Depot. In October 1978 he contacted Julian Thompson to confess: 'I was the driver who, in conjunction with the conductor concerned, used to pass through Streatham Change Pit non stop when proceeding from the north. Considered in retrospect, this procedure would appear to have been highly irregular and not a little fool-

hardy. It was fortunate indeed that the act was not witnessed by anyone in an official capacity, otherwise no doubt prompt disciplinary action would have resulted. However, all went well, the operation being always effected without mishap.

Not only the crews had their eccentricities, the passengers came in all shapes and sizes as well. Some well known regulars were featured in a newspaper article on 28th March 1950. Headlined *Aboard The Charladies Special*, the text focussed on the lively journey to work of some very necessary workers:

The photographer's flash illuminated the front of the tram, some transport officials and some fog. It was 5.36am, and the 84 tram should have left Camberwell Green for Westminster. As the flash went off there was a yell inside the tram and a woman banged on the window. 'Put our pitchers in the paper,' she invited me and the photographer. The Mrs Mopps of South London were in the Charladies Special that takes chars to government, newspaper and legal offices. Most of them have sat in the same seat for over 10 years. 'Sit down mate,' said 63-year-old Lionel Savage to me cosily. For 40 years he has been a conductor at Camberwell Green and a regular on the Charladies' Special.

'Palace of Varieties' called out the conductor we were at the Houses of Parliament. At the end of the Embankment the last lady left, telling the conductor he could have his tram when she won the pools. The conductor found some knitting on a seat. 'Catch,' he called to Miss Ivy Eagle of Iverton Road, Peckham, a passenger for 18 years. 'All right, I'll get it tomorrow,' she called back. The tram returned to Camberwell.

Whilst the House of Commons may have attracted the wry humour of the Charladies Special, the 'performers' at the *Palace of Varieties* were regular passengers on the night trams. All-nighters served the Victoria Embankment and would ferry constituency MPs back to Battersea, Clapham, Tooting, Camberwell, Lewisham or Catford. The Kingsway Subway provided a link for those members who had homes in North London. The last northbound 35 left Westminster at 12.20am to reach Highgate Archway Station at 12.58am. An article in the November 1951 issue of the *London Transport Magazine* describes the nocturnal experiences of several staff. Conductor Bill Rymill, aged 66, was quoted as saying that when he served on the late night 35, he would wait for a group of MPs who were mostly back benchers – 'and a jolly good crowd, always laughing and joking' – they were then conveyed through the subway to be dropped off near Russell Square where many of them used to stay in hotels.

Another conductor, David Profit from Holloway Depot, recalled in an interview with the author that crews normally had a good relationship with their regulars, especially charladies and printers. He also

remembered taking the fare of actor Robert Beattie, who travelled on his 35. Another actor, the young Richard Attenborough took the starring role in a film adaptation of the Norman Collins novel *London Belongs to Me*; to enhance the action, Sidney Gilliat, the director, took possession of the lower deck of an E/1 tram as it shuttled between Balham and Clapham South. These scenes which were filmed on 13th March 1948 unfortunately ended on the cutting room floor!

Other celebrities recalled by Conductor Profit were prize racing pigeons which were

transported in three crates on the driver's platform! It is worth stating that front platforms offered an alternative freight service for parcels, sacks, pushchairs, baskets of flowers etc. which could be ferried at the motorman's discretion. Normally a fee of 2d was charged for this service. Many a working man who could not afford a horse and cart would use the tramway system as a distribution network, but this useful facility came to an end with bus conversion.

Life on the trams was routine but never dull.

1951

THIS WAS a sombre year for London's tramways, as trams and well established routes disappeared with frightening speed, so that by the end of the twelve months large areas of South London were completely tramless. The final night of routes 2, 4, 6, 8, 10, 20, 22, 24 and all-night service 1 came with Stage 2 on Saturday 6th January. The number of trams withdrawn totalled 101, to be replaced by 117 buses working new routes 50, 57, 57A, 95, 104, 155B, 155W 189, 189A and 287. Route mileage lost at this conversion was around 20 (32 km), and the following areas were now covered solely by buses: Wimbledon to Tooting, Balham High Road, Clapham Road, Mitcham Road, Southcroft Road, Mitcham Lane and the Albert Embankment. The overhead section, originally part of the London United Tramways, from Wimbledon Broadway to the change pit at Longley Road, Tooting was abandoned, together with the complicated junction at Tooting Broadway. Only the 630 trolleybus route remained to supply electric street traction along Garratt Lane and Mitcham Road. As it was, the last route 10 car which left Tooting at 12.21am on 7th January managed to get itself stuck on a dead section of conduit at the Broadway, and perforce the conductor had to raise the pole to use the 630 trolleybus overhead in order to resume the journey. The last 10 was crewed by Driver Robert J. Miles and Conductor Kenneth Frost who headed back towards Norwood Depot. The passengers on this last car were treated to an exhilarating ride from Streatham to Brixton at a speed certainly well in excess of the norm for this route.

Other valedictory festivities involved Car 1847 which left Wimbledon at 11.42pm and was the last northbound tram to use Tooting change pit. It was packed with an estimated hundred enthusiasts. At 16 minutes past midnight, the official last tram, Car 1829, sponsored by the Balham and District Chamber of Commerce, left Tooting Broadway. It was accompanied by Territorial motor cyclist

Travelling by tram in 1951 – the lower deck of a former West Ham tram features in this view of a passenger boarding at New Cross. The conductor is standing on the rear platform, ready to assist if need be. Note also that one of the lower deck panels adjoining the letter T in the fleet name has parted company from the main body frame. It is hoped that this particular car will last until July 1952, long enough to see out route 46.
V. & J.Farlie

Above New Year's Day 1951 in Westminster Bridge Road, and Car 2054 on route 16 battles through the snow and slush. J.H.Meredith

Left This is the last night of route 1, an all-night service which was replaced by bus 287. Car 2107 was withdrawn to Penhall Road after performing this valedictory run. G.F.Ashwell

Facing page top On 6th January 1951, the last day of route 2, Car 1848 reverses on Long Road crossover, Clapham Common. This section of track was formerly worked by route 34 which had succumbed in Stage 1, and was kept 'live' for short working cars, as seen here. Note that part of the Common has been given over to prefabs to alleviate the postwar housing shortage. Wherever it was possible, it was part of LCC thinking to erect these buildings on sites near a tram or bus route. J.H.Meredith

dispatch riders from the Royal Corps of Signals. Later six brewer's dray horses were harnessed to the tram with white tape, as a symbolic gesture harking back to the horse car days. Another historic echo was that this stretch of track formed part of the first LCC conduit line, opened in May 1903. Car 1829 with Driver J. Stapleton and Conductor W. Levitt reached the depot at 1.45am.

Clapham Depot was now closed to trams and the remaining cars from the 1777–1851 series were transferred to New Cross. They replaced a number of E/1s including 'rehabs' which were sent for scrap. Telford Avenue also lost its ex-MET Felthams which were shifted to Penhall Road pending their collection by Leeds City Transport. The ex-LUT Felthams were retained for service on routes 16 and 18, as was ex-LCC Car 1. Norwood Depot gained several E/3s which were also allocated to routes 16 and 18. In fact during this period the main Croydon trunk routes were operated by four depots: Norwood, Brixton Hill, Telford Avenue (North Shed) and Purley.

Car 1847, the last service 2 car, is pictured on its valedictory journey. It is grossly overloaded with what may be termed 'boisterous well-wishers'. The presence of a number of police officers and LT officials failed to prevent souvenir hunters preserving at least some of Car 1847's artefacts before it headed to the scrapyard. Unfortunately, the partial demolition of 1847 was ill-timed, because London Transport still needed this tram and repairs had to be effected! It finally reached Penhall Road in October 1951. LT Museum

February and March 1951 saw a number of minor permanent way renewals. The inside curve at Westminster was relaid and new points were installed in Plumstead High Road. On Monday, 12th March, alterations were effected at Victoria terminus. Route 78 was to use the southern island, and routes 54, 58 and 66 were to terminate at the northern island. In fact, to be more precise, cars on route 66 had to pick up passengers almost at the end of the track, whilst routes 54 and 58 picked up at the Vauxhall end of the northern island.

As regards the replacement buses of Stage 2, the folk of Wimbledon started getting restless over the new 155 service. It seems on one Saturday morning a correspondent of *Modern Tramway* noted seven

Left Streatham change pit was one of three to be abandoned during 1951. Car 2059 waits for the usual routine of being 'ploughed up' before advancing on to the conduit equipped tracks leading to central London. It is worth noting that this location was positioned right in the middle of the main London to Brighton trunk road, the A23, but in this era, the early 1950s, there is plenty of space for what amounts to a trickle of vehicular traffic.

Below The points have just been changed for Car 199 as it heads south into Lambeth Palace Road. For those with a broader interest in road transport, the tram is being pursued by a single deck Green Line coach.

consecutive buses passing through High Street, Merton, in the direction of London, full up, not stopping, and leaving people waiting at stops. Confusion also developed over the crews' inability to cope with new B and W suffixes (which signified via Blackfriars or via Westminster), and many 155s turned up with the wrong indicator blinds, thereby adding to the passengers' frustration. Local residents in Clapham and Streatham were also getting fed up with the prolonged conversion work on the former depot sites. London Transport could only apologise, and put the delays down to national shortages of building materials such as bricks, cement and steel, and they also blamed the bad weather of the 1950–51 winter. It was also noted on 5th March that rebuilding work had commenced at Camberwell and New Cross. In the case of the latter, some trams had to be moved out to Penhall Road which they used as a temporary running depot.

Stage 3 took place on the night of 7th/8th April and involved Croydon area routes 16, 18 and 42. This stage saw the end of operation over tracks formerly owned by Croydon Corporation Tramways. Members of the LRTL were out early on the last day, and for their farewell tour they first joined Car 1 at Highgate. A stop was then made in the Kingsway Subway *en route* for Brixton, Streatham and Purley This rather special tour car was ably crewed by Instructor Stan Collins and Conductor Trembath of Telford Avenue Depot. After reversing at Purley, Car 1 went back to Streatham, making a detour via the Thornton Heath branch on the way. Ex-LCC Bluebird Car 1 was then run into Telford Avenue Depot prior to being driven across South London to Penhall Road, there to await transport to Leeds.

The party of tram enthusiasts was then treated to an outing on Feltham Car 2079 which had been specially retrieved from Penhall Road for the occasion. The first port of call was the City terminus at the northern end of Southwark Bridge, and from there via the Elephant and Castle to the new County Hall roundabout. There then followed a spirited ride along Lambeth Palace Road and the Albert Embankment, over tracks last used on 6th January by routes 22 and 24. This section of 'abandoned' track was retained as an emergency access route to either Victoria or Westminster Bridge, in case of a major blockage at either Kennington, Stockwell or Westminster Bridge Road. Car 2079 then visited Victoria for the last time, before making the return journey to Telford Avenue, where the tour ended. *Modern Tramway* noted: 'the tour was characterised by a delightfully informal atmosphere, quite unlike that of previous tours.'

Above Let it not be said that the sun always shines in South London. Here in damp, gloomy conditions, which many thought (unfairly) suited the trams, Car 193 makes its way along Balham High Road. W.J.Haynes

Below Felthams were shipped north by Pickfords. Trucks and running gear were placed on the flat bed of the lorry, whilst the car body was transported on the low loader trailer. Car 2132, former LUT 363, received its third fleet number as Leeds 569. D.A.Thompson

In the evening, Stan Collins was similarly employed in driving Car 947, hired by the Streatham Ratepayers' Association to mark the end of tramway operation in the area. Proceeds from the sale of tickets went to charity, although London Transport pocketed £4 for the hire fee of the tram. This practice came in for some criticism from the *Croydon Advertiser*, who berated LT for their 'monumental meanness', especially as good causes would benefit from the special cars. The second private hire tram of the evening was car 839, which was hired by the Croydon Chamber of Commerce and ran from Purley to Thornton Heath Pond. Driver Bill Stout and Conductor Arthur Allen received a ceremonial send off by Walter Troake who rode the first electric tram from Purley to Norbury on 26th September 1901. Another passenger was Tom Basten, a former conductor, who remembered seeing the first horse tram in Croydon on 9th October 1879. As was to become normal for each stage of the aban-

donment process, hundreds of people lined the streets to say farewell to their local trams.

Early on 8th April a number of the 375–399 series cars left Purley for further service at New Cross Depot. *En route*, Car 391 damaged its plough carrier outside Telford Avenue and had to be pushed by Car 378, which was the last tram to leave Purley Depot. This nocturnal cortege reached Kennington, where the order was reversed and Car 391 was towed the rest of the way to New Cross Gate. An enthusiast on the gate at Penhall Road noted on 8th April that amongst the extra trams in the yard were 40 Felthams and Car 1 (all destined for Leeds), and ME/3 Car 1444 (destined for the bonfire). All in all, a total of 92 trams disappeared at stage 3 to be replaced by 106 buses working new services 109 and 190. Another casualty of this stage was Purley Depot which was effectively replaced by the rebuilt Thornton Heath Garage.

Some of the flavour of tram routes 16/18 is given by Gerald Druce:

'The tram route followed the main road (A235 and A23), providing a short cut to some suburban railway stations. Hence the London bound morning peak hour loading which consisted of two types of regular passenger. Some went all the way to London on the tram, as the Embankment served a wide stretch of the main area of employment. A transfer to a Kingsway Subway car (on the same ticket) further increased the region served. This made economic sense even when working a six day week. The tram fare from Norbury Station was 11d return (with extensive transfer facilities) – a total of under £4 for three months compared with some £5 for a quarterly rail season (plus extra for the tube). In the 1945–50 period the fare structure still reflected the pre-London Transport era. There was a specific 4d workmen's return only available in Croydon e.g. Norbury to Croydon, Greyhound – just over three

Facing page As can be observed in this scene, Streatham High Road has been widened, but no money has been forthcoming to realign the tram tracks. Consequently, trams would often seem to snake across the carriageway, which caused some confusion for oncoming traffic. Car 1910 is about to go the wrong way round a Keep Left island, and eccentric behaviour like this did not endear the trams to other road users. When the rails were lifted, a new dual carriageway was built. LTPS

Above Two tramcars pass the Half Moon at the corner of London Road and Handcroft Road, Croydon. Car 202 is working service 18, whilst car 1911 is on the local route 42. The centre alignment of the overhead has caused the off-set trolley poles of both trams to reach left. J.H.Meredith

Right The last day special tour is pictured at Purley.

miles each way. The normal fare was 4d single. Another case was the local penny ha'penny and tuppenny ha'penny transfers. Since the highest value ticket 1947–1950 was 7d some long journeys would require two tickets, but in practice very few people would go by tram from Croydon to London.

The Southern Electric rail service from Norbury and Streatham was good – Norbury had nine trains an hour to Victoria and three an hour to London Bridge. Streatham had six an hour fast to London Bridge and three an hour to Holborn Viaduct. Thus the trams also carried many short distance passengers who required penny ha'penny or tuppence ha'penny tickets to these stations. This made hard work for the conductors on a crowded tram, and occasionally a driver would 'drag the road' (dawdle) to give his mate more time.

The length of route between Croydon and Purley was a particular loss, as the good condition of the Croydon tracks plus the performance of the Felthams made this stretch a favourite ride for enthusiasts. Features of note also lost in this conversion were the single track and loops sections of the Thornton Heath route, which even included some interlaced track in Brigstock Road.

Brixton Hill Depot was cleared of trams by 7th April. This was almost the last chapter in the story of this 'white elephant' building which had been opened in 1924, and had been under-utilised since – at one stage in the mid-1930s the whole building had contained just two trams. A double change pit was installed on the entrance track and overhead wires were used inside the depot. Telford Avenue Depot eventually emerged from a period of reconstruction as Brixton

Bus Garage. The only other reconstruction in April directly relevant to the tramway system was the relaying of the Charing Cross and Savoy Street crossovers on the Victoria Embankment.

Two diary notes from Julian Thompson add some local colour to the usual run of events. On the evening of 14th April, whilst waiting at Westminster tram shelter, a New Cross car was spotted with its axle box on fire. This particular defect was known as a 'hot box', and although relatively uncommon, a tramcar so stricken could only be driven *very* slowly. As there was a marked lack of lay-bys where the car could be left to cool down before lubricant could be applied, the offending vehicle would perforce hold up all those trams trailing behind.

The other rare sight was noted on Saturday 21st April at Manor House, where two route 33 cars were observed using both tracks at the terminus, it being normal practice for only one terminal track to be occupied. It is worth remembering that the terminus of route 33 was actually the former change pit which was situated south of the road junction. Prior to 8th May 1938, tram route 41 had continued northwards on the overhead.

Several regal occasions were celebrated in London – on Thursday 4th May, King George VI opened the Festival of Britain on the South Bank site. London Transport had put

out much publicity for visitors, but the mention of tram services was only very cursory. The emphasis was now firmly on the bus side and eight special bus routes were inaugurated in connection with the Festival. It was obviously a hectic time for King George and Queen Elizabeth, because on Tuesday 8th May, the King and Queen of Denmark paid a state visit. The processional route caused some disruption to tram traffic, but trams continued to use Vauxhall Bridge Road. In order to shift the crowds afterwards, trams were despatched, fully loaded – 74 seats per car, four at a time. Also at times of street closures for state visits, cars could be turned short on the new County Hall roundabout. This was not without its dangers, as an official notice to drivers explains:

'Several accidents have occurred recently where Addington Street, Lambeth adjoins Westminster Bridge Road. A Tram Pinch sign has recently been erected in this vicinity, but all drivers, particularly those operating tramcars, are requested to exercise special care when traversing this thoroughfare.'

This instruction was no doubt in the minds of motormen when, on Tuesday 5th June, Westminster Bridge was closed on the occasion of the state visit of the King and Queen of Norway. For two hours a procession of trams terminated at County Hall round-about. Tracks along Newington Butts and Kennington Park Road, disused since 7th April, were reopened for route 33 cars to reach the Elephant. Notices were posted at tram stops in Kennington Road (the normal 33 route) to inform the public that, from 2.30pm, trams on route 33 would be diverted.

During late spring the Felthams had been leaving Penhall Road to make the road journey to Leeds. By June, 66 type UCC cars had arrived, and 42 were noted in service. LT Car 1 was renumbered 301 in the Leeds fleet, and was offered in replacement of cars 2144 and 2162 (scrapped in May) which were fire damaged at Brixton Hill Depot. In fact, there was an embarrassment of riches for the northern city, because by July ex-London trams were arriving so frequently that the works was unable to deal with them. There-

fore, some Felthams found themselves stored outside Torre Road Depot before being converted to Leeds' specifications

Other events in June included track renewals on Dog Kennel Hill, Bostall Hill and Basildon Road. In fairness to London Transport it would seem that the PW department did not put off vital work and it must be noted that the tracks on Dog Kennel Hill were due for abandonment in October.

The next stage of the abandonment process took place in midweek – on Tuesday 10th July, to be precise, when routes 68 and 70 were replaced by bus routes 188 and 70. Also for the axe was the short lived extension of route 72 to Hop Exchange; cars on this route were then cut back to a crossover on the Embankment at Savoy Street. In fact the Hop Exchange terminus had masqueraded under several names, and it was also listed as Borough and London Bridge. Names aside, Car 208 bound for New Cross Gate on route 72 was the last car to leave Hop Exchange at 11.17pm on the night of the 10th.

Inevitably the celebrations centring on routes 68 and 70 delayed the departures of the last cars from Waterloo and Tooley Street respectively. Crowds of Londoners turned out to witness Bob Mellish MP and

various members of the local TGWU pay homage to Car 587, the last 70 from London Bridge to New Cross Gate. It was an occasion of nostalgia mixed with anticipation for the future, and it was evident from the speeches, that both MP and union men considered that progress was being made, and that the new buses would give a better service for the working people of Bermondsey, Rotherhithe and Deptford. No doubt the worthy members of Bermondsey Borough Council could now sleep better, knowing that the problems of paving and bad track had been at least partly solved.

Route 70 was part of London tramway folklore and it was probably the post-war tram service with the most character. Even the fact that the rebuilt Creek Bridge was taking shape, and tramlines were not wanted on the new structure, somehow added to its unique reputation. It had attracted literary attention when, in early 1951, Lucy Masterman had published her book *London from the bus top*. In spite of the obvious fact that tram route 70 hadn't quite succumbed to its diesel competitor, the whole of the chapter devoted to the 70 was filled with historic details of the buildings and sights encountered *en route*. The author recounts quite correctly that the area of the Surrey Docks

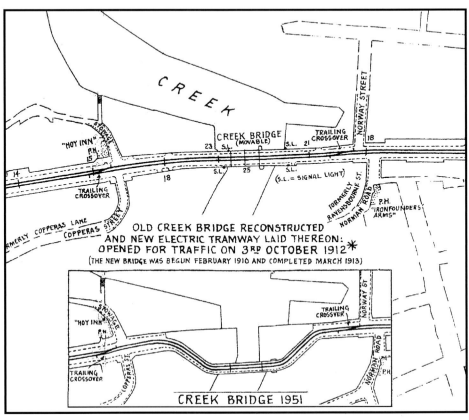

had suffered badly from bomb damage, as had many of the houses, public buildings and churches in the Jamaica Road and Rotherhithe districts. Evelyn Street, traversed by routes 68 and 70, was steeped in a tradition going back to John Evelyn, Samuel Pepys and the naval history of Deptford. The end of the line was at Church Street, Greenwich, only a stone's throw away from St Alphege's Church, built by Hawksmoor, and the Wren-inspired Royal Naval College.

The statistics of Stage 4 reveal 33 trams withdrawn, replaced by 38 buses. The system had now shrunk to 65½ route miles (104 km) and 129 track miles (206 km). The demise of routes 68 and 70 should have taken place at Stage 7, but this was swapped with Stage 4, mainly due to the situation with Creek Bridge and the fact that Stockwell Bus Garage was late in opening because of difficulties in rehousing people from the site.

More statistics were quoted by *The Star* on 2nd August. (In general *The Star* had a more sympathetic view towards public transport than its competitors – politically, it was more left of centre.) It maintained that the removal of London's trams had given rise to more congestion, because to match the seating capacity of the trams, more buses were needed. At the same time London Transport had issued a set of figures showing the average speed of trams, including stops, to be 10¼ mph (16 kmh) – just one mile per hour short of the central bus average. *Modern Tramway* noted that, even under adverse conditions imposed by track layout and age of the rolling stock, London's trams still held their own in the face of LT propaganda about the alleged greater speeds of the replacing buses.

The Festival of Britain on the South Bank site came to an end on 20th September. On the opposite side of the Thames, the only incident of note connected to the Festival occurred when powerful floodlights were being fitted to the underside of Waterloo Bridge. These had the effect of dazzling tram drivers as they emerged from the southern portal of the Kingsway Subway on to the Victoria Embankment. Jane Drew, the architect of the Riverside Restaurant, was supervising this unwelcome illumination when she was politely requested by two policemen to direct the beam elsewhere. Meanwhile, a tail back of trams had formed in the tunnel. Obviously they were all shy of being in the spotlight!

Visitors to the Festival could study a few tramway exhibits which had been included in the Transport Pavilion. These included a working truck and electrical equipment from Blackpool Corporation, plus several one-sixteenth scale models contributed by Richard Elliott. Mr Elliott, one of the most active

Above Car 566 is a member of the 'slow' series of E/1s particularly associated with routes 68 and 70. Note that the track on Creek Bridge has been immaculately laid in a modern road surface. What a contrast to granite setts and uneven paving! – it shows what the PW department could achieve given the will and the money.
R. Hubble

Below After the demise of routes 68 and 70, it seemed that the area was devoid of tramways. This was not the case, as the railway track laid in Grove Street, Deptford, still saw the odd locomotive hauled train from Deptford Wharf on the former London Brighton & South Coast Railway, to the War Office Reserve Supply Depot. This steam tramway was opened on 15th December 1900 and perished in the mid-1950s.

members of the Tramway and Light Railway Society, was employed as a technical assistant at Charlton Works. His model-making skills were featured in the April 1951 issue of the *London Transport Magazine*. The article described the meticulous and painstaking work involved in creating an accurate miniature replica of an LUT type Z open topper which was to be exhibited at the Festival of Britain.

On 30th September, Driver A. E. Sharman of Camberwell Depot, and Conductor L. W. Parkes, presided over an LRTL tour where trolleyless HR/2 Car 120 was hired for an extensive jaunt which took in the Dulwich routes due for imminent closure. Car 120 also visited Manor House, Brixton, Old Kent Road, and tracks along Albert Embankment and Kennington Park Road which had been retained for emergency use. Part of this tram marathon included trips to the two change pits at Downham and Woolwich. Since the car was equipped for conduit operation only, it was unable to explore any overhead wire sections. Motorman Sharman demonstrated various driving techniques including coasting, running on only one pair of motors and using the run back brake.

The HR/2 operated Dog Kennel Hill routes passed away on 6th October. Tram routes 56/84, 58, 60, 62, 66 and all-night

Above Car 120 is depicted in Short Street at the Elephant and Castle. It is about to join the southbound track in Walworth Road. Short Street was unusual in that trams ran against the direction of other motor traffic. Consequently it was designated a One Way Street – Except Trams! J.H.Meredith

Below The 84 from Peckham Rye has just beaten Car 1857 to the right of way along Grove Vale. There was originally a triangular junction here at Goose Green, but the north to east curve from Lordship Lane into East Dulwich had been disconnected by the 1940s. On the pavement outside the shops is a temporary 'dolly' tram stop which may indicate that this is a last week scene of the Dulwich routes.

Above Peckham Rye terminus lay in a pleasant, leafy suburban road with very little other traffic. HR/2 rehab Car 1887 waits for Car 1888 to move from the stub at the entrance of Stuart Road.

Below There is plenty of movement at the triangular junction of Brockley Rise with Stanstead Road. Car 102 will proceed straight ahead, after Car 1423 has swung past to reach its terminus at Forest Hill. Car 1872 waits on the other side of the traffic lights to follow the 66.

service 7 were replaced by bus routes 184, 185, 176A, 176, 36A and 286. The most prominent feature of this stage was of course Dog Kennel Hill itself; double track on the grade opened for electric traction in 1906 and was quadrupled in 1912. No two trams were to occupy the same track on the hill in case of brake failure. The sound of HR/2 trams descending the hill lives on in the memory of many enthusiasts and older local residents, and the application of the magnetic brakes on the down grade was one of the most evocative sounds on the post-war system. The replacing buses were but poor recompense.

Trams withdrawn totalled 99, and these were replaced by 109 diesel buses. But even this figure hides the fact of the considerable loss of passenger capacity – 99 HR/2 cars equalled 7326 seats, whilst 109 buses of the RT/RTL type could only manage 6104 seats. One can only assume that this was deliberate policy in the face of LT calculations that there was substantial over – capacity on the tram services.

Twelve of the 101–159 series of trolleyless HR/2s were transferred to work route 35. The rest of the class went to Penhall Road, and were later scrapped. The other batch of HR/2s soldiered on from New Cross, taking the place of older E/1s which then made the one way journey to a fiery end. Included in the last round-up were the majority of the former Clapham E/1s (1776–1851), which actually preceded some of the oldest of the class to the scrapper's torch. Also the ninetieth and last Feltham to be sold to Leeds, Car 2158, was despatched on its journey up north. Camberwell Depot, by now renamed Walworth Garage, ceased to run trams and their allocation of 21 vehicles for route 35 was switched to New Cross Depot.

The last tram from Blackwall Tunnel terminus was Car 145, and as had become customary on these occasions, it was given a good send off by a crowd of locals and well wishers. The valedictory celebrations lasted into the wee small hours and it was noted that Car 1893, from Catford, arrived at Camberwell Green at 2am. Also on the last evening, P J. Davis, a well known South London tramway enthusiast, hired Car 120 for a farewell tour.

Passenger services also ceased on the peak hour extras worked by route 36 from Woolwich to Catford via Greenwich South Street, Blackheath Hill and Lewisham Road. This connecting link between Lewisham and Greenwich was not immediately abandoned and it remained energised; it was retained so that staff cars for Charlton Works could avoid the detour via New Cross. The link was finally decommissioned in January 1952.

On the face of it, the conversion scheme seemed to be going well, and London Transport was in self congratulatory mood, when in the October issue of *London Transport Magazine* it published a leader on the half way mark of Operation Tramway. Headed *A First Class Job*, it mused on the fact that 200 miles (320 km) had been abolished in a year and that everything reflected 'the high standard of efficiency that London Transport has set for such major traffic operations.' The cover picture of the magazine was an attempt at a symbolic representation of the half way stage. It featured two crew men looking back wistfully on Car 1395 which was marooned on one of the Penhall Road sidings.

Of course, there were always those unwilling or unable to share LT's optimism. In a letter to *Modern Tramway*, R. M. Jenkins expressed his views on the recent conversion:

'The buses on service 185 run every ten minutes in off peak periods, whereas the trams had a four minute headway [*actually a six minute headway – author*]. A London Transport regulator remarked that people are sometimes unable to board vehicles at midday, a state of affairs hitherto unprecedented. A tramcar, he said, acts like a dredger and eliminates the queue . . .' It would seem from this letter that the RT and RTL type diesel buses were still lacking in their ability to transport crowds and to clear the queues.

Remembrance Day fell on Sunday 11th November, and motormen and conductors who were ex-servicemen, were encouraged to wear medals and decorations on this day. Two minutes silence at 11am was also observed throughout the country and trams were halted as a mark of respect to the fallen. At the end of the two minutes, drivers were instructed to use only half power so that a current surge did not overload the electrical sub stations. It was also recorded in the November Traffic Circular that tram crews should draw the attention of inspectors to heavy falls of leaves on the line, so that they could be cleared from the rails promptly.

The end of 1951 and the Christmas period was rather an anticlimax for the trams. Even the press seemed to have tired of reporting

every accident, and the story of a derailed tram on 15th December merited only brief mention in one of the evening newspapers. The Christmas schedule was similar to years gone by, with the obvious difference that there were now fewer tram routes. It is worth noting that the all-night routes 5 and 35 were still providing a regular service over the festive season, except on Christmas Night/Boxing Day morning. Those partying late in town on Christmas Eve could get a tram at half hourly intervals from Savoy Street to Downham Way on route 5. Revellers leaving the Embankment at 1.21am could expect to be in New Cross by 1.46am and at Downham Way by 2.08am. An hourly service was also run between Archway and Bloomsbury, Southampton Row on route 35.

Thus an eventful year ended. On 1st Jan-

Above To avoid the railway station at Forest Hill, the main tram route took a looped detour via Devonshire Road and Waldram Crescent. Car 1866 climbs Devonshire Road in the direction of the station. O.J.Morris

Below An interesting characteristic of route 58 were the single track and loops sections in Lewisham Road and here at the beginning of Greenwich South Street. There were no signals and, except in thick fog when inspectors acted as human tokens, motormen relied on line of sight for safe passage. Car 143 heads for Greenwich, whilst Car 1863 waits by Blissett Street to resume its journey to Lewisham. R. F. Mack

uary 1951, a total of 650 trams were called upon to operate Monday to Friday schedules. At the end of the year this number had dwindled to 323, all of which neatly sums up the depressing situation. The new year of 1952 would see the demise of the system.

MISHAPS

ROAD TRAFFIC accidents occur in every city and London during the tramway era was no exception. Most contretemps affecting the system were highlighted by the local press and the feeling grew in some quarters that trams were a major cause of traffic disruption. This unfair view was enhanced by the fact that derailments and collisions sometimes seemed to follow one another in short order, giving the impression that the system was rapidly falling apart. On the other side of the coin, buses and trolleybuses also had their fair share of misfortune.

It must be borne in mind that, in wet weather, a road surface of tramlines edged by granite setts was very slippery. This fact contributed to a number of accidents, but the major cause of death and injury to tramway passengers was the reckless habit

Facing page The passengers on this early morning Workman 72 got more than the usual thrills and spills when Car 576 gathered speed down Grand Depot Road, Woolwich, derailed at the Anglesea Road crossover and went headlong into the Co-op on Woolwich New Road. A woman and three men were treated in St Nicholas's Hospital for minor injuries and shock. The removal of the unfortunate tramcar on 18th April 1946 involved the severing of the upper and lower decks. Car 576, now the only single deck E/1, was then hauled off for storage at New Cross Depot, never to re-emerge in passenger service.

of motorists attempting to drive between the tramcar and the kerb at tram stops. Some 'hotheads', particularly along the route from central London to Streatham and Croydon, could regularly be observed intimidating alighting passengers and forcing others to make a hasty retreat to the pavement. This dangerous practice of passing a tram on the inside at stopping places had already been outlawed by many countries, but it was not until the appearance of the June 1992 *Highway Code* that it became an offence in Great Britain.

The technology of the London tram also contributed to its own downfall. The conduit system became increasingly accident prone, and a jammed or broken plough could tie up the service and produce delays. Whilst a derailment on overhead equipped routes could normally be dealt with quickly and efficiently, the opposite was true on conduit sections. Here, any tram that came off the track usually managed to damage its plough or carrier. The upshot of all this was predictably a long queue of tramcars waiting to pass the stricken vehicle. Several duty inspectors would then have their work cut out to marshall the tram traffic coming the other way so that single line working could be instituted past the obstruction. All of which was very time consuming and detrimental to the 'image' of the tram.

The year of 1948 produced its crop of accidents which of course were manna from heaven for tramway abolitionists. On 6th January, at Longley Road change pit, Tooting, a conductor was crushed to death. He was standing between two cars when a third tram collided with back of the second. According to the official enquiry, the motorman of the third tram blamed the accident on the partial failure of his magnetic brakes. On 24th March 1948, an eastbound 38 left the track at the points outside St Alphege's Church, Greenwich. It careered over the kerb on to the pavement, and tragically killed a man in a wheelchair. Nature intervened on 14th June, when a tram on route 46 was struck by lightning by Well Hall railway bridge, Eltham – no casualties were reported. In the following month the heavens opened again and Lee High Road was

Below What do you do with a smashed tram which is holding up the service? One hopes the inspectors have got this one under control. Some 46s and 44s going in the Woolwich direction will have to be diverted via Westhorne Avenue whilst Car 1951 remains stuck outside the Odeon, Well Hall. The obvious solution seems to be to shunt the car round the corner and then back down Westhorne Avenue in the direction of New Cross Depot. In the event, the tram was placed temporarily on one of the tracks circulating Well Hall Roundabout, and route 72 trams had to reverse round it until the breakdown tender arrived. R.Hubble

flooded, effectively severing routes 46 and 72 which had to be worked in two sections either side of the inundation.

Several derailments in the summer were followed by a serious smash at Bridgefoot, Vauxhall, when E/1 Car 1611 on service 28 ran into the back of E/1 Car 1353 on service 78. Eight people were hurt and seven were taken to St Thomas's Hospital. On 18th October, a 33 tram in Green Lanes hit a lorry with such force that it caused fatal injuries to a lady pedestrian. At the end of November and beginning of December, a typical London 'smog' was held responsible for two accidents. In Grand Depot Road, Woolwich, two trams, two lorries and a cyclist were involved in a pile up, whilst in Tunnel Avenue, Greenwich, a tram, a motor cycle, a van and a coach found themselves magnetically drawn to one another.

The motorman's lot was not a happy one when Charles Tomkins appeared in court on 4th January 1949. He testified that, as driver of a 33 tram in Green Lanes the previous October, he sounded his gong when he saw a lorry on the tracks in front of him, but unfortunately failed to apply his brakes in time. He was fined forty shillings (£2) plus three guineas (£3.15) costs for his part in the fatal accident.

Another tram driver falling foul of the law was Henry Upcott of Battersea who was censured by a jury for not driving with due care and attention. A verdict of accidental death was passed at the inquest on Mrs Fanny Martinelli (75), of Kennington, who stepped out in front of Driver Upcott's tram in Clapham Road. The rails, explained Mr Upcott, were greasy due to earlier rain, and it was difficult to stop the tram as quickly as it would have been normally.

January's mishaps also included a 68 tram which collided with a heavy lorry laden with sugar. Although the track in Tower Bridge Road was blocked for 40 minutes, it is not recorded what happened to the lorry's cargo. Later in the month, another lorry got itself sandwiched between two tramcars in Queen's Road, Peckham. Fortunately, nobody was hurt.

The police were called out on Monday and Tuesday of the week beginning 6th February. Route 68 tramcars operating through Bermondsey and Deptford were the subject of attack from an air rifle. Several windows were broken and one passenger sustained cuts from flying glass. The investigation from the local constabulary failed to find the culprit for this act of reckless vandalism, which was especially serious because trams were not equipped with safety glass.

On 26th March, E/1 Car 1597 collided with a petrol tanker on the north side of Battersea Bridge. Both vehicles suffered fire

damage, the front of the tram was burnt, but Car 1597 was repaired in May and returned to service. During the night of 29/30th a burst water main in Newington Butts caused all trams to be rerouted by Walworth Road, and the disruption lasted long enough to affect all-night services as well. A tram and a bus collided at the junction of Westminster Bridge Road and Kennington Road on 27th April. Two bus passengers, suffering from shock, were taken to hospital, and the tram driver, John Bird of Camberwell, was also injured. Traffic was held up for half an hour.

On 14th August, a 64-year-old woman, alighting from a tram at Kennington, was knocked down and fatally injured by a car driven by Dr Kenneth Rothwell of Folkestone. Although Dr Rothwell did not stop after the incident, and in spite of testimony from a tram inspector and a bystander that the unfortunate victim was 'knocked the whole length of the tram', the coroner was satisfied that there was no evidence of culpable negligence. He recorded a verdict of accidental death.

During August and September 1949 both tracks opposite Temple Station, on the Victoria Embankment, were relaid. This did not attract press coverage, unlike the continuing stories of summer accidents: on 25th June a tram, a coach, a private car and a taxi were involved in a crash at Camberwell New Road. Trams on both tracks were held up for 24 minutes. Cars on routes 54, 58 and 66 were diverted via Walworth Road. On 10th August, trams on six routes were delayed when a car on the 34s ran into some plough problems at the junction of Blackfriars Road and Surrey Street. Further anguish was recorded on the 26th of the month when a car on route 6 derailed at the junction of Kennington Road and Kennington Park Road. The breakdown crew must have got there quickly, because the delay to other services was only six minutes. It is worth recording that just over 150 trams an hour used this particular junction, and a few yards south of this location at the Kennington Gate junction, the peak hour frequency was almost 250 trams an hour. On 15th September, the Old Kent Road was blocked for 15 minutes when a horse drawn van pulled in front of an Abbey Wood bound tram on route 36 and caused a collision. Later in the same day, a lorry inconveniently broke down on Eltham Hill, delaying passengers on routes 44 and 46. A derailment on Saturday, 24th September, saw car 2069 come to grief a few yards beyond Charing Cross Bridge on the Embankment. A jammed plough was the cause of the delay and the breakdown crew had soon removed the car's track brakes and had jacked the vehicle up. The Feltham was then attached by chain and rope to a break-

down tender and gradually manoeuvred back on to the track.

On 23rd August, motorman Eric Young of Catford was fined twenty shillings (£1) with the customary three guineas costs, for knocking a boy off his cycle in Plumstead High Street. In his defence, Driver Young maintained that the tramlines were only 2ft 8in (813mm) from the kerb, and he thought the boy had taken notice of his warning gong. Seven days later the northbound track of the Kingsway Subway was blocked for 15 minutes when the trolley pole of a 35 tram fouled the subway roof. On the same day, a car on route 8 broke its plough carrier on Stockwell Road, and for half an hour cars on routes 8, 34 and 78 had to be diverted.

A minor step in the campaign promoting accident prevention occurred in the August traffic circular, when drivers of route 33 trams were reminded to give hand signals when entering and leaving the single track section by Burma Road, Green Lanes.

The London daily and evening press continued their accounts, much to the embarrassment of the tram department. Indeed, the papers had a feast day on 26th November when headlines announced – *Four Trams In Crash. Women Among 13 Injured. Eleven Routes Held Up.* The reporter went on to describe the chaos of the four-fold tram collision at Elephant and Castle, thus: 'A No. 34 southbound tram ran into the back of a No. 84 going to Forest Hill. The 84 was in turn knocked on to a No. 16 and that on to a No. 36. The two rear trams were the most severely damaged, having taken the force of the impact.' Again, many of the injuries were caused by flying glass and one of the conductors was seen with blood streaming from his face. Unfortunately, this was not the end of the year's toll of troubles. On 21st December, a 52 tram and a 10 tram collided at the junction of Southwark Bridge Road and Southwark Street. The newspaper noted that 'dozens of other trams were delayed.' The year ended with a *Two Hurt In Triple Crash* headline – a tram, a bus and a lorry ploughed into one another on Coldharbour Lane, Brixton. The hapless tram driver, P R. Connell of South Lambeth, held his New Year's celebrations as a patient in Kings College Hospital. Of course it was unfair to single out the trams for lurid press coverage, especially as road traffic accidents involving other vehicles were occurring on a daily basis all over the metropolitan area.

One has to be sorry for poor old Driver Eric Young, he of Plumstead High Street single track fame, who again hit the headlines on 10th January 1950, when he was explaining his actions leading to the death of an 87-year-old man who fell in front of his tram on a dark, moonless night. Driver Young said

In August 1950 a car driver and his passenger had what eye-witnesses described as a 'miraculous escape' when the car in which they were travelling was trapped between a northbound and a southbound tram outside Croydon bus garage. The car was overtaking one tram and tried to cut in front of the second approaching from the opposite direction, resulting in it being sandwiched between the two. The car driver and his passenger were taken to hospital with multiple injuries after being cut free from their squashed vehicle.
John Gent collection

on a 16 tram when a fuse blew and caused some smoke. The current was switched off for thirty minutes on the down track (from London), and eighteen minutes on the up track. Trams on three routes had to reverse either side of the defective car. On 13th February, Julian Thompson records in his diary:

When I reached Lambeth Baths (Lambeth Road/Kennington Road) in the evening, there was a queue of cars. No. 2094 had become derailed on the up track. The rear bogie had ridden over towards the down track, but the front bogie was on the rails. It was in such a position that all four tracks were blocked. Car 2094 was moved a little north, to allow the 12s through. After about 20 minutes the breakdown tender arrived, and rerailed the pony wheels by a tug with a chain, and the car moved forward to rerail the drivers.

The next day a route 6 car derailed at the junction of Marshalsea Road and Southwark Bridge Road. Trams were turned either side of the obstruction, and some were diverted via the Elephant and Castle and Blackfriars Road.

On 3rd March, a service delay occurred when there was a power failure in the Angel area of North London; this led to all trams and trolleybuses being inoperative for 11 minutes. Eleven days later, George Elliott, driver of a 56 tram, was knocked unconscious in a collision with another tram in Blackfriars Road. Both cars were going in the same direction until the front tram on route 16 stopped at the traffic lights at Stamford Street. An inspector on the back platform of the first car received minor injuries. It must have been one of those days, because over at Vauxhall trams were delayed a quarter of a hour by a fractious passenger who wouldn't pay his fare. The conductor called a policeman and the one-man protest against higher fares was continued at the nearest police station. More time was wasted on 17th March, when tram routes 36, 38 and 40, plus trolleybus routes 696 and 698 were halted by a lorry which had become jammed in Beresford Street, Woolwich. This was a narrow, busy thoroughfare with double track that filled the carriageway, leaving restricted space between the outer rails and the kerbs, and although the street was supplied with several crossovers, it seems a shuttle service

that the front lights of trams were still fitted with a shield as in wartime, consequently they did not give much illumination of the road ahead. Black-out shields had to be fitted quickly at the beginning of the war. A mask to restrict light emission was put over the headlight of every tram. It was combined with a glass slide which produced a rear red light. Before September 1939, the rear light was part of the route number stencil fitting beside the staircase. Examination of headlamps after 1945 showed that a different headlamp mask was used in peacetime – LT was most indignant at accusations that the black-out fitting had been retained. All the

same, it is still a mystery why LT did not simply revert to full pre-war illumination standards as was the case with other British tramways which survived the war.

The jury returned a verdict of accidental death, adding a rider that the lighting and condition of the tram track in New Kent Road could be improved upon. The foreman of the jury remarked that this rider on the condition of the tracks was based on observations at the spot of the accident.

On 9th February, several people were injured when a route 12 bus collided with the rear of a tram on Westminster Bridge. On the same day there was a minor contretemps had to be worked either side of the obstruction. The final hold up of the month happened on the twenty-first, when a large bolt got stuck in the conduit slot along Southwark Bridge Road. Tram services from the Southwark Bridge and Hop Exchange were affected.

Icy conditions may have been to blame for an accident on 28th April, when a tram proceeding along Stockwell Road collided with a lorry, sending it through a shop window. Three people were injured. The next day, a defective conduit point tongue at New Cross Gate was the cause of several broken ploughs and a 30 minute delay in the tram service.

The months of May and June had their fair share of accidents. On 9th May, a 36 tram ran into the back of a car on route 40 by Church Lane, Charlton. On 23rd May, cars on route 34 were held up at Clapham when a lorry broke down blocking both tracks. Passengers were transferred to buses, and the obstruction was cleared in 15 minutes. Unfortunately at the end of May the fates were particularly unkind. A tram on the Victoria Embankment near Charing Cross Underground Station struck and killed Edward Thomas, aged 60, of Brixton. In the afternoon of the 30th May, the Embankment saw another incident as the magnetic brakes on a Croydon bound car seized up near Waterloo Bridge. Over at the junction of Coldharbour Lane and Denmark Hill a tram split the points and caused other trams a half an hour wait before they could get past. The first week of June began with a heatwave and the effects of this were immediately felt on Lavender Hill, Battersea. On the afternoon of 6th June, a plough caught fire and filled a tram with smoke. The damaged vehicle was removed and there was a hour's delay in the service. Worse was to follow as the mercury in the thermometer climbed. The castings holding the conduit conductor T rail expanded with the heat and forced the T rail downwards out of reach of the ploughs. A trackwork gang had to open the conduit to prize the rail back into position. Between the Town Hall and Clapham Junction around 180 feet (55 metres) of conduit was also affected, and it took the PW crew three hours to remedy the situation. Single line working was instituted during the remedial work.

On 13th June, five passengers were injured when a 38 going to Abbey Wood and a 35 bound for Highgate collided in Westminster Bridge Road, outside Lambeth North Station. About 50 trams were held up for half an hour. Disaster struck again on the 19th, when pedestrians jumped for safety as a 78 derailed at the junction of Brixton Road and Stockwell Road. The tram came to rest

at the kerb. Another derailment was on 30th June, when Car 2140 at the Horns, Kennington, blocked the curve into Kennington Road. It was a firm belief amongst some enthusiasts that standards had slipped as regards tram driving – lack of expertise and judgement contributing to the number of slow speed collisions.

There was no service at all between Lewisham Town Hall and the Clock Tower, when on 8th July, a power failure stopped trams. Cars on route 54 were diverted via Brockley, and those on service 58 reversed either side of the dead section. Order was restored in 15 minutes. On the same day as tram lights went out in Lewisham, E/3 Car 192 went over the top at Westminster. Its plough jammed and it left the tracks to veer across the loading island into a passing taxi. On 22nd July, three were hurt when a bus and tram collided head on in Falcon Road, Battersea. Both vehicles were badly damaged and the bus driver had to be cut from his crushed cab.

August 1950 was a bad month for collisions. On the second day of the month, a 38 tram and an excursion coach bound for Margate collided in Woolwich Road, near Tunnel Avenue. On 7th August there was almost a repeat, when a tram in Lewisham Way was derailed by a motor coach, bound for Eastbourne this time. Three people received minor injuries on 10th August, when an 84 tram collided with a 36 at St George's Circus. A 74 ploughed into the back of a 54 tram at Downham Way on 14th August. On the same day in Camberwell New Road, a 36 bus hit a route 40 tram going to Greenwich. The next day, five tram routes were delayed 27 minutes when a car on route 38 broke its plough carrier in the Old Kent Road.

The most spectacular mishap of the month happened on the 23rd, when Car 1396 got out of control on Cedars Road, derailed at the junction with Lavender Hill and careered into Hemmings Bakers Shop. Two passengers and the driver, S. W. Castle from Wandsworth Depot, were injured. Mr Castle was trapped for a time in the wrecked tram. Tragedy also struck tram conductor, Peter Bull, who was killed on the same day. Conductor Bull was leaning from the front platform of his tram in Vauxhall Bridge Road, when he was hit by a tram going the other way. On 24th August, a 78 West Norwood bound tram left the rails in Brixton Road and came to a standstill at the kerb. There was a 53 minute delay on both the up and down tracks. Trams on the up track were turned short at Angell Road, and at Atlantic Road on the down track.

Away from public thoroughfares, the damage reports during October and November 1950 included six trams which were

burnt in a fire at Brixton Hill Depot. Felthams 2162 and 2164 were badly affected.

On Tuesday 17th October, a car on route 48 struck a route 2 bus in Norwood Road, Herne Hill. The tram completely wrecked the rear platform of the bus and top deck passengers had to wait a quarter of an hour until LT gangs could release them. A similar incident happened on 8th November, when a bus and tram collided in Peckham Road, Camberwell. Again, the staircase of the bus was crushed and firemen had to organise the escape of the trapped passengers by means of the emergency exit and several ladders. On the same day, G. E. J. Hornsby, driver of a 58 tram, had to be freed from his car after a collision with a coal lorry at Catford Bridge. He sustained injuries to his legs and feet, and was detained at Lewisham Hospital.

An army tank transporter collided with a tram in Woolwich Road, Charlton on 3rd January 1951. The rear of the tram was damaged, but there were no reported injuries. Across in Brixton, Mrs Yeuldon, aged 50, was less fortunate when she was wedged between a 10 tram and a 59 bus. She was attempting to board the tram at the time of the accident. The next day brought three separate incidents of tram fires. E/1 Car 1312 burned out in Balham High Road as it was on tow after a breakdown. The fire lasted 10 minutes and caused some traffic disruption. On the Victoria Embankment near Temple Underground Station, passengers made a quick exit from a tram and firemen had to put out the flames with a hand extinguisher. Finally, snow at the Elephant and Castle was believed to have caused a short circuit which resulted in at least one plough fire. Services were again held up whilst the stricken vehicle was removed from the scene.

On Sunday 7th January 1951, as the replacing buses of Stage 2 were taking to the streets, E/1 Car 1386 was disabled outside Oval Station with a broken plough. Trams then worked wrong road across Oval junction and regained the right track in Camberwell New Road. Later in the day, two trams broke down in Harleyford Road, and a 54 was obliged to use the wrong track in Vauxhall Bridge Road. A breakdown of a more personal kind, one between London Transport and Streatham's courting couples, reached the papers on 16th January. It seems that the niches of the disused Gaumont Cinema had been inadvertently illuminated by LT's floodlights on the car park opposite where new buses were stored. Obviously the site of the former Telford Avenue Depot had not yet been rebuilt, and the only excuse an official kill-joy could offer was that 'to keep an eye on our buses we have flooded the street with powerful lighting.'

On 7th February, a tram derailed in Holloway Road, causing long delays. Another derailment happened on 16th February, when E/1 Car 1818 came off the iron whilst traversing the little used curve from New Cross Road into Queens Road.

On 26th June, Car 143 collided with a motor car on Westminster Bridge. The unfortunate vehicle was then pushed into a 33 coming in the other direction. The driver of the motor car, P. Williamson of Bridlington, and his passenger, were extricated from the 'tram sandwich' and taken to St Thomas's Hospital. Perhaps it is worth noting that, as an 'out-of-towner', Mr Williamson may not have been aware of the London motoring tradition of steering well clear of the two tram tracks nearest the kerb on the northern side of Westminster Bridge.

August 1951 was enlivened by the headline *22 Hurt In Lambeth Crash*. A 153 bus and a 56 tram had collided with such an impact that the tram had been derailed and the bus had had its side ripped off. The reporter also added that: 'the tram was believed to have crossed the points in the wrong direction [sic], hit the bus, ripping it open and tearing off its rear wheels!'

A chain dangling from a passing lorry caught in the conduit at Camberwell Green, thus causing a short circuit. This occurred on 17th August and six tram routes were delayed from 8.55am to 9.15am. In spite of the narrow width of the conduit slot – originally three quarters of an inch (19mm) and later widened to one inch (25mm) – small objects and street refuse could accumulate under the roadway, and could easily foul the T rails which then shorted out the traction current, as happened at Camberwell Green. PW workers were equipped with long handled mirrors which they inserted through the conduit slot to check on faults. This process was repeated every 15ft (13.7m), and if a cracked insulator or other fault was detected, the ganger then informed the substation and the current was turned off while repairs could be effected. Normally other detritus was swept clear from the bottom of the conduit and the nearest hatchway was then lifted for the rubbish to be removed.

Since Stage 1 of the conversion scheme, tram replacement buses had been operating along the Embankment over the track nearest to the bank of the Thames. This had caused some minor collisions, but matters came to a head on 11th September, when an RTL bus working route 170 emerged from Temple Place and was struck by a 56 tram heading towards Blackfriars. The bus was thrown on its side and 20 people had to be taken to hospital. Fate struck again on 27th September in a bizarre rerun of the previous Embankment accident. This time a 38 tram collided with a 170 bus. The tram then left the rails and struck a furniture van which in turn hit a passing lorry. It must be remembered that bus route 170 was the old 31 tram, and as such could not use the Kingsway Subway. These accidents led to a change in the method of operation from Temple Avenue, whereby buses ran a short distance along the Embankment before crossing to the tram tracks.

Route 38 was previously in the news on 11th September, when a car derailed on the points at St George's Circus. Some trams were turned back at the Elephant, whilst others were diverted via Westminster. The delay lasted eight minutes and affected routes 36, 38, 56, 74 and 84. On 13th September, two passengers and Conductress Lilian Obbard were injured when a 54 tram ran into the back of a 52 tram on Bromley road, Catford. On 25th September, it was the turn of a 52 to ram a 40 at New Cross Gate. Passengers were injured by flying glass, and relays of ambulances took casualties to the Miller General Hospital, Greenwich.

The final year of London's trams was not that old when on 29th January 1952, under the headline *Tram wrecked lorry – 10s. fine*, the story unfolds of Driver Charles Homewood of Herne Hill. He was hauled up before the magistrates for completely wrecking a three ton lorry. The unfortunate lorry driver maintained that he passed the traffic lights at green, but as his vehicle crossed the tramlines, he saw a tram coming towards him very fast. The impact of the crash wrenched off the back axle of the lorry and ripped the body from the chassis. In his defence, Motorman Homewood said the lights were green for him and he was going very slowly. The interesting thing about this court case was the inability of the witnesses to judge the speed of the oncoming tramcar. Enthusiasts are sometimes guilty of exaggerating tram speeds, but it seems that in 'Homewood's Tram versus Lorry', not even the police could supply reliable evidence.

Thus this sad category of untoward events drew to a close and with the demise of the system on 5th July, railbound vehicles could no longer be blamed for road traffic accidents.

THE FINAL YEAR: 1952

WE COME to the last fateful year of London's tramway system. To be strictly accurate, it was London's first generation tramway network that was about to become defunct. In 1952, the idea that electrically powered vehicles running on rails would eventually return to the streets of the capital, would have been greeted with expressions of stark disbelief by the public

Saturday 5th January 1952 – last day of routes 48 and 52. On Southwark Bridge, Car 2043 works the last 52. Car 167 will then reverse and perform the honours as the last ever midday 48 from the City. Route 48 was cut back to St George's Church on Saturday afternoon. Note the offset conduit on the bridge roadway.
J.H.Meredith

transport establishment. The editorial staff of *London Transport Magazine* mirrored the party line in the February issue. 'Proof Already' shrieked the headline, and a whole string of well rehearsed phrases spun out of the publicity machine. Readers were told that new replacement bus services were achieving far greater regularity than was possible with the trams. Indeed, the greater mobility of buses had altered the situation drastically, so much so that (I quote) – 'traffic conditions in Croydon High Street, which is narrow and a notorious black spot, have been *completely transformed*' – (my italics). Congestion was also said to be on the decrease and queuing times had been

reduced, in short, all was sweetness and light – a perfect justification of London Transport policy. The only blot on the landscape was the nine remaining tram services, and the reader was assured that they were not long for this world.

Certainly the February article was biased, but whether this slant was occasioned by misplaced enthusiasm or deliberate distortion of the facts to fit the LT world view is unclear. Whatever the reason, the optimism of congestion-free roads from the suburbs to central London vanished within months of the final withdrawal of tramcars. In the early 1950s the word on most road transport planners' lips was 'flexibility', but one won-

On Norwood Road by Trinity Rise, there was a short stretch of single track. Car 1942 approaches cautiously, the motorman on the alert for oncoming vehicles. This particular car was obviously normally used on route 33, as it retains its Kingsway Subway stencil. *N.Rayfield*

ders why so few of these experts, both inside and outside London Transport, seemed to grasp that this flexibility might swing both ways. Few pundits appear to have figured out that public transport users would later vote with their feet and use their new found affluence to purchase private cars which would then replace the bus as the most comfortable and flexible form of transport.

However, we are getting ahead of ourselves and we need to return to the opening month of the year. On 5th January, Stage 6 of the abandonment programme was carried out. This resulted in the loss of 109 trams and the withdrawal of routes 48, 52, 54, 74, 78 and all night service 5. They were replaced by bus routes 48, 149, 69, 179, 178 and 285. Victoria, Vauxhall, Grove Park, Loughborough Junction and Catford now joined the ranks of tramless areas. No more would cars inch round the single tracks in Milkwood Road and Poplar Walk Road, nor would a seemingly endless line of trams swallow test match crowds from the Oval. The traffic stopping manoeuvre of cars swinging out across the carriageway at Loughborough Junction on route 48 was in the past, and the rails along Downham Way, one of the last tramways built by the LCC, fell silent and acquired a veneer of rust.

The withdrawal of routes actually commenced at the northern end of Southwark Bridge on the afternoon of Saturday 5th January, when Car 2043 left at 2pm on the last

52. It was scheduled to arrive at Grove Park at 2.54pm. Obviously, as this was the last journey from the City, progress was delayed somewhat, and it was nearer 4pm when Car 2043 finally reached New Cross on the return from Grove Park. As the dusk of a winter's day turned to night, many tram riders took a last nostalgic farewell, and it was noted that business was brisk at Victoria terminus. Car 1920 working the 54 was the last tram to leave Victoria in the early hours of Sunday 6th January. Next to Driver H. Mayo on the front platform was 70-year-old William Gould, who had driven the first electric tram across Vauxhall Bridge some 45 years previously. Amongst the other 'last nighters' was Conductor P. Howes, who

probably had trouble getting all the fares in before Car 1920 reached New Cross Depot. Car 1996 did the honours as the last 48, with Car 1998 seeing out route 78.

There is a story attached to Car 1998 – it was actually driven by G. Harry Guilmartin, whom we shall meet later in connection with the closing of the Kingsway Subway. Mr Guilmartin was formerly a motorman at

Below left Victoria prepares to give the last car a good send off in the very early morning of Sunday 6th January. *J.H.Meredith*

Below Car 1998 nears the end of its run as the last service vehicle on route 78. The 'last nighters' seem to have left at least some of the light bulbs on the top deck, but the side route boards have already disappeared.

93

Above Stage 6 of the conversion programme saw the demise of the ex-Walthamstow trams. Amongst other well known characteristics, they were always readily identifiable by the deep wooden windscreens. Here at the Yorkshire Grey roundabout, a member of the class is working route 72. Its trolley wheel is about to cross the skate which will activate the overhead frog. The next skate a few yards down the road will alter the points so that the car can veer left into Westhorne Avenue. R.Hubble

Clapham and Telford Avenue depots. In the early hours of Sunday morning, he got the regular driver to give him a chance to drive the last 78. The journey ended at Norwood.

After this stage, all the ex-Croydon E/1s were taken out of service, and the same fate befell the ex-Walthamstow cars, with the exception of cars 2055 and 2056 which were retained for transporting workers to the CRD, thus the two fastest cars were kept for the staff! Most remaining standard E/1s found their way to Penhall Road. Car 1025 was granted a reprieve and was sent to Charlton Works for a thorough overhaul before being transported by road to Reigate Bus Garage. There it was joined by ex-West Ham, four wheel balcony Car 290. Both trams were set aside for preservation purposes, and at the time of writing are now prize exhibits in the London Transport Museum at Covent Garden.

Car 2 and many of the 552–601 series of E/1 class were still active. Amongst the trolleyless HR/2s, 33 had gone for scrap, leaving just cars 118, 121 and 122 working route 35 which was confined to conduit tracks. The fleet now consisted of classes E/3, ex-East Ham, ex-West Ham, and members of class HR/2, series 1853–1899. Depots in use were New Cross (routes 35, 36/38, 40, 46 and 72), Norwood (route 33), Abbey Wood (routes 36/38, 44 and 46), and Holloway (routes 33 and 35). Route mileage was 46 (74km), of which approximately 25 per cent was equipped with overhead wires.

There is a school of thought which maintains that the closer to abandonment the trams came, the faster they were driven. Certainly there is evidence to confirm that in the last few months of the system some drivers threw caution to the winds. Let Fr Benedict Sankey take up the story:

I was waiting at the stop opposite Penhall Road, and had a much longer wait than usual. Eventually a tram appeared, stopped, set down a passenger and took me aboard. It then continued up to town, driven flat out and only stopping where there were passengers to be set down. This must have been infuriating to people left behind at the other stops, but the driver was surely quite right in aiming to get back on schedule, which would benefit those further in towards London. But there were other occasions when there didn't seem to be any reasons for speeding. I did wonder whether they were aiming at keeping the same frequency with fewer cars – with drivers taken off to train for buses – and of

The end of the line for route 33 was on the southern side of the important Manor House junction. Car 1949 is very much an intruder in trolleybus territory. B.T.Cooke

Past the famous statue of Queen Boudicca in her war chariot, Car 1989 turns on to Westminster Bridge.

course by that time there were all those E/3 and HR/2 trams available. Or were the tram men setting out to show the bus people what a tram could do? On one run down the Old Kent Road I was on a 36 or 38 which overtook a 63 bus at the beginning of that thoroughfare, and passed the previous 63 at the other end of it!

The State Funeral of King George VI took place on 15th February, and at most workplaces the employees had time off from 12 noon to 3pm. Trams ran as normal, with the possible exception of ex-East Ham Car 91 which was noted on the approach track to Charlton Works. It was marooned outside the gate with a bad case of jammed gears. Luckily the staff worked wonders with this particular car and it soldiered on until the final day of the system.

Later in February, Lewisham Borough Council revealed that it was having some qualms about tram track removal. John Carr, the Lewisham Borough Engineer, was quoted as saying that it cost £10 to tear up every yard of disused double tram track. He also estimated that the council might have to pay £10,000 for the removal of tramlines in London Road, Forest Hill. Although he went on to state that payment by London Transport plus money from the sale of scrap steel would cover the £168,000 Lewisham was obliged to spend on track lifting in the borough, he intimated that the council was still concerned that it would be have to fund any shortfall.

An interesting proposal which might have

halved Lewisham's costs came in the House of Commons. Mr Steward, Conservative MP for West Woolwich, through whose constituency ran routes 44, 46 and 72, suggested that after tramway abandonment the outer tram rail nearest the kerb be left in place. This would then form a guide to motorists to aid them in foggy conditions. The Minister of Transport then promised to give the idea careful thought, and there the matter rested.

On Sunday, 2nd March, the fares went up again! Some fare stages were altered to conform with a rationalisation process, and this resulted in some unfortunate passengers having to pay double for their journey. This situation outlived the trams and was partially remedied by the government on 31st August when certain of the March increases were pegged back to a more reasonable level.

At the end of the month the weather turned nasty and snow storms affected the capital's roads. Trams continued to operate, being aided by the efforts of crews operating snowbrooms, but there was considerable disruption to routes 33 and 35 north of the River Thames. At the time it was said that all available snowbroom works cars had 'gone south', as it was considered there was a low probability of snow! However, as we shall see, this assessment of the situation was not quite accurate.

April 1952 was noteworthy for the closure of the Kingsway Subway. A deed which was castigated by the LRTL as the crowning folly of the conversion programme. The subway, which dated from 1906, was opened for double deck operation on 14th January 1931. The tunnel services had been worked by E/3 cars. A notice was fixed to the top deck

The northern approach to the Kingsway Subway as enthusiasts like to remember it. Many still wonder why London Transport allowed this mass transit connection under central London to be closed. The ramp in Southampton Row still exists at the time of writing. B.J.Cross

Left The countdown to the end of a London tramway institution has begun. The motorman of a northbound 35 glances at an inspector's time card in this highly atmospheric scene of the Kingsway Subway.
Chris Ware

Right Passengers make their way out of one of the tram stations. With the closure of routes 33 and 35 this direct and useful traffic link was lost. One wonders how many ex-tram passengers bothered to transfer to the replacing bus routes which were soon to be caught up in the surface traffic around Aldwych and The Strand.
Chris Ware

bulkhead doors which informed passengers that they were permitted to use the front, driver's platform to alight at Holborn or Aldwych tram stations. At both locations there were island platforms, thus boarding or alighting through the rear of the tramcar was not feasible.

However, before the big show, a little known event occurred on 3rd April, when snowbroom 037 was the last single decker to pass through the subway. It was driven by G. Harry Guilmartin, former tram driver and, at that time, an LT bus inspector. As it was a chilly night, the regular crew was easily persuaded to spend their time in the lower saloon out of the icy blast, whilst Inspector Guilmartin and tramway photographer Frank Jones stood on the open platform. Car 037 was then duly driven across South London to Penhall Road.

Routes 33 and 35 were replaced by bus routes 171 and 172 on 5th April. The all-night 35 from Southampton Row to Archway Station, Highgate, was abandoned in favour of bus service 292. The subway was obviously not suitable for diesel bus operation, and routes 171 and 172 had to follow a different course from Aldwych to the Embankment. Fifty-two trams were withdrawn and these included a large number of the ex-Leyton E/3s, series 161–210, and perforce the last few trolleyless HR/2s (all remaining tram routes had some overhead sections). Also on the slippery slope to oblivion were many HR/2s of the 1854–1903 series, and inroads were made at the same time into the 552–601 series E/1s.

On the last day of the Kingsway Subway routes the LRTL organised a tram tour using two ex-Leyton E/3s, cars 195 and 199. The itinerary is depicted on the map opposite, drawn by John Meredith. One hundred and forty members and friends participated, and amongst the guests was George Utting who witnessed the opening ceremony of the LCC electric tramways on 15th May 1903.

Other special guests later that evening were catered for by special hire trams, and these people included a veritable galaxy of civic dignitaries, all eager to see the trams out in style. The last northbound 35, the 11.55pm from Westminster to Highgate, was Car 185 crewed by Driver Alfred Keir and Conductor John Howes, the latter was a par-

A packed Car 185 is about to say farewell to the Kingsway Subway. This ex-Leyton E/3 subsequently saw out its days on the remaining South London routes and finally met its end at Penhall Road in December 1952.

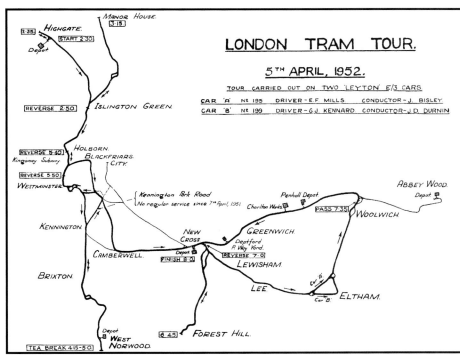

LONDON TRAM TOUR.

5TH APRIL, 1952.

TOUR CARRIED OUT ON TWO 'LEYTON' E/3 CARS.

CAR 'A' №. 195 DRIVER - E.F. MILLS   CONDUCTOR - J. BISLEY
CAR 'B' №. 199 DRIVER - G.J. KENNARD   CONDUCTOR - J.D. DURNIN

ticularly efficient individual as he collected every fare on the car, creating record takings of over £26. At Holborn Tram Station former Inspector Paddy Walker, who had previously done 24 years service in the 'tunnel', came out of retirement to send Car 185 off towards the slope up to street level. Not everything went according to plan and on the ramp leading to Southampton Row, Car 185's circuit breakers blew, but swift action by a passenger on the rear platform prevented the car rolling back to Holborn Station. Needless to say, the tram was packed with passengers, estimates giving the total at around 100, which might account for Car 185's reluctance to climb the one in ten (10%) gradient. Ken Glazier was on this particular vehicle and he recalls the incident:

I was on 185 standing crammed at the front of the lower deck (I couldn't get upstairs!) and recall the frisson caused by the loss of power. As we crawled up the slope, there was a crowd of sightseers straddled across the tracks at the top and one of the inspectors on board shouted to the driver 'Mow 'em down!' Fortunately his resolve was not tested as they moved away in time – but we did not stop.

THIS LAST TRAM OUT OF NORWOOD Showing
WILL CARRY THE MOVIETONE NEWS
SHOWING THE FIRST THREE PAST THE
POST IN THE GRAND NATIONAL 1952

REGAL
NORWOOD
FROM TOMORROW

W NORWOOD
CHAMBER OF
COMMERCE

W NORWOOD
CHAMBER OF
COMMERCE

GOOD BYE OLD 33 GOOD BYE

Above Ex-Leyton E/3 Car 210 went straight from its valedictory run on the 33 to a storage track at Penhall Road, where it awaits the attentions of workmen with sledge hammers and cutting torches, but first has its commemorative inscriptions recorded by a photographer. LT Museum

Below Trams wait in Norwood Depot for the last round up. The roll call reads from left to right: snowbrooms 018, 022 and 028, rail grinder 02, ex-Walthamstow 2056, E/3s 2000 and 1990, and finally stores van 03.

Going in the opposite direction to Car 185 was Car 173 from Theobalds Road to Westminster. This particular vehicle was hired by Holborn Borough Council and contained the mayor and local bigwigs. Meanwhile south of the River, the Mayor of Lambeth Mrs Elsie Lyon Boltz had her first and only taste of tram driving, as under the watchful eye of Driver James Sparke, she piloted Car 197 for some of the way from Addington Street to West Norwood. Contemporary newspaper reports give us a flavour of the evening:

Two trams left Addington Street in the farewell ceremony. The first was the last scheduled 33 tram crammed with ordinary passengers who had queued hopefully for several hours. Many were turned away. The Mayor's tram, which left a few minutes afterwards, was filled with councillors and other civic notabilities. At the Oval, a dozen eager hands rushed to help the pointsman guide the tram towards Brixton. By this time nearly a dozen private cars had joined the procession, sounding their horns at every opportunity. A police car, weaving in and out of the traffic, joined in the fun. Groups of people among the 500 at Brixton tried to strike up Auld Lang Syne as the quarter-mile procession came into view, but they were drowned by the cheering.

A location long associated with the trams, since 1906 in fact, was the Victoria Embankment. Car 1939 heads for Westminster in the last few hours of the system.

And what was happening inside the tram? Nobody knew, for the lights went out, and when the retinue arrived at Norwood Depot there were no electric bulbs, no bells and no 33 number boards anywhere to be seen. The souvenir hunters had been busy. And so the carnival of fun came to its end with the Mayor breaking a bottle of beer over the last car.

Mr Jimmy Madden, who opened the depot 42 years ago, saw all the cars depart for the breaker's yard at Charlton . . . and then the depot closed for the night, and for good.

An interesting aside from all this nostalgic merriment was the fact that London Transport seemed to he making a profit from the last tram industry. The standard charge for each 'special' had now risen to £8 16s, which was more than double the price charged at the Croydon conversion. All of which left even less for the charities which had been supported by local Chambers of Commerce. Obviously the criticism levelled at London Transport and its 'monumental meanness' had had as little effect as the campaign to save the system.

Another 'last nighter', also charged at the premium rate, was Car 210 which was decorated by members of the West Norwood Chamber of Commerce and ran from St Luke's Church to Brixton. It then returned to Norwood Depot where Driver Bill Bassett and Conductor Percy Rutland took a ceremonial farewell from Depot Engineer Jimmy Madden. Mr Madden was featured in the May issue of *London Transport Magazine*. His biographical details were impressive: 74 years old and 42 years in charge of maintenance at Norwood Depot. The closure of the depot marked the end of his life's work, two small consolations were that the bulk of the Norwood E/3s would be transferred to New Cross for further duties, and that Norwood Depot was not converted to a bus garage.

After the official celebrations had ended, a low key, but just as poignant, moment was enacted by Driver Tom Fitzpatrick as he drove Car 184 through the subway. This was the last of some 13 cars to be cleared from Holloway Depot, which now became all trolleybus. Also on board Car 184 was tramway historian John Barrie. He stayed on with Driver Fitzpatrick as far as Westminster, where a New Cross crew took over for the last stage of the journey. The gates at both ends of the Kingsway Subway were then closed. An exceptional and unique transport facility had been lost.

Also sacrificed were the last two tram routes in North London, and for the first time in many decades there were no trams at the Angel, Islington. Brixton, Herne Hill and West Norwood became bus only preserves and the change pit at Effra Road was abandoned. One final note: the text of one official LT notice pasted at Aldwych Station began 'Trams routes cease to operate through this subway after Saturday 5th April' – underneath somebody had chalked one word – *WHY*?

Now that Stage 7 had been completed, attention turned to the remaining six routes. Bouyed up with the success of the previous conversions, London Transport had decided in February to amalgamate the last two planned stages, which resulted in routes 36/38 joining the others in Stage 8 rather than hanging on until October. Although trams still served the Embankment, Westminster Bridge, Blackfriars, the City, St George's Circus and the Elephant, the attention of many enthusiasts was drawn away from the familiar locations towards what was happening in South East London.

Above On 1st July 1952, at another famous London tramway landmark, the Elephant and Castle, Car 1953 on route 38 has stopped on a dead section and must wait for a following tram to nudge it gently forward. Meanwhile, a 36 passes in the direction of New Kent Road. J.H.Meredith

Below On the right of this view in Greenwich is the National Maritime Museum and Greenwich Park. On the left is the Royal Naval College which borders the Thames. The traffic situation in this area today has become critical with very high pollution levels. The days when trams supplied quality, environmentally friendly public transport now seem very distant. N.Rayfield

Throughout May and June, especially at weekends, there always seemed to be several tramway buffs permanently stationed outside New Cross Depot, Charlton Works and Abbey Wood Depot. As if in response, security at these sites was tightened up, the official view being that unauthorised persons on LT property were a danger to themselves and others. The powers that be were especially mindful of the rebuilding work at both depots which resulted in piles of debris heaped next to partly filled-in inspection pits – truly traps for the unwary. But, human nature being what it is, not even the mandarins at 55 Broadway could prevent the steady disappearance of 'souvenirs'. One hesitates to say there was a black market in tramcar fixtures and fittings, but research has revealed that a number of serious tramway archaeologists were determined to augment their collections before the objects of their desire were consumed in the Penhall Road conflagrations. For those who had some spare cash, George Cohen Sons & Company Ltd of Broadway Chambers, Hammersmith, would certainly do a deal. The firm had been contracted by LT to scrap its tramway assets. The market rate for a gong was two shillings and sixpence, and a single seat could be purchased for five shillings. Indicator blinds, controller keys, destination boards and number stencils were also to be had at a price. However, there were many

enthusiasts who either did not have income to spare, or were so anti-London Transport's tram scrapping policy, that they regarded anything they could salvage as 'fair game'. This removal of heavier items such as controllers and trolley heads would later prove a blessing for the tramway preservation movement, and many ex-LT items found their way on to restored tramcars which now operate at various heritage museums.

Another centre of tramway interest was Beresford Square, Woolwich. Here amongst the stalls of the street market, one could while away the hours by observing trams on all the remaining routes. Outside the historic Royal Arsenal Gate there passed a procession of cars on routes 36, 38 and 40, plus a number of trolleybuses on routes 696 and 698. On the opposite side of the Square, by a handily placed public convenience, a single set of rails played host to cars on routes 44, 46 and 72 which terminated on a loop formed by Green's End and Woolwich New Road. At peak periods when the queuing pens by the Arsenal Gate were full of homeward bound workers, almost a hundred trams an hour traversed Beresford Square; adding to the feast of electric traction was a very frequent service of trolleybuses bound from Woolwich, Parsons Hill to Erith, Bexleyheath and Dartford – thus even in the last months of the system there was still plenty of activity, and it was hard to believe that this was all about to pass into oblivion.

Time moved relentlessly on to the last week of the system. As is well known, all vehicles, save the ex-West Ham cars, carried a long poster on each side advertisement panel. This read:

LAST TRAM WEEK

and underneath in smaller red letters:
ON JULY 5 WE SAY GOODBYE TO LONDON.

Special tickets were issued for the last week, which of course were retained not only by enthusiasts, but also by disinterested members of the travelling public who could spot them as mementos to show the grandchildren. On the reverse side of each ticket was a picture of a horse tram, vintage 1861, and drawing of an E/3 car. Cleaning staff at the two remaining depots also had occasion to bless the special tickets – tram floors had never been so uncluttered, nor used ticket boxes so empty as in the week of Sunday 29th June to Saturday 5th July.

In many ways the increased passenger loads transported during this time only served to accentuate the unreal nature of the last few days. It seemed everyone wanted just one last ride. Londoners and those from out of town could be seen forming queues at tram stops throughout most of the day and also into the formerly quiet times of midevening. The trams were doing what they

Above The trend towards taking a nostalgic last ride degenerated into something of a frenzy on the final day of service, Saturday 5th July 1952. Nowhere was this more apparent than here on Victoria Embankment where queues of people scrambled aboard every available tramcar.

Below In the final week of operation the conductor went about his business as normal, with the exception that the different coloured tickets he dispensed were retained by many as keepsakes. In spite of its impending demise the interior of this tram still looks fit for a few more years service. Note that even on a fine summer's day, the average Londoner of 1952 still shows a marked conservatism in his or her attire. Cloth caps are still very much *de rigueur*.

did best – carrying large numbers of people efficiently, and one may add, not contributing to the pollution level on the streets. This fact went largely unnoticed and unreported. Environmental considerations did not rate high on the political agenda at the start of the 1950s nuclear age, and contemporary reports by motor engineering experts were confident in reassuring the public that they had nothing to fear from well maintained petrol and diesel engines.

Regular travellers who relied on the trams to get to work or to go shopping were rather miffed by the crowded conditions, and the fact there there did not seem to be enough trams around. For this fleet deficiency London Transport must take the responsibility. Having publicised the last tram week and encouraged Londoners to take their last nostalgic rides, its officials then proceeded to withdraw trams from service during the week, thus aggravating the situation. Many totally serviceable E/3s and HR/2s were put to the torch at Penhall Road in June, and these vehicles could have helped. However, staff and trams made it to Saturday 5th July, which dawned a fine summer's day, perfect for photography, ideal for the youthful tram spotters, who, armed with their pocket edition of Ian Allan's *ABC of London's Transport Part II – Trams and Trolleybuses*, would carefully cross out the number of every tram witnessed in service. There was a festive, almost carnival atmosphere as trams passed with valedictory inscriptions chalked on the side, most of which lamented the passing of an 'old pal'. Together with the normal traffic sounds there was the crunching noise as car after

Far left On the southern side of the Square there was the terminal loop for routes 44, 46 and 72. Car 309 runs slowly towards the points which are set for the return via Woolwich New Road. The rails running straight ahead behind the photographer form a connection with tracks in Plumstead Road. This was used for trams working to and from Abbey Wood Depot. R.Hubble

Left A few yards on from the previous view, we encounter the interlaced points at the entrance to Woolwich New Road. These were originally installed by the LCC in 1910 to avoid excessive property demolition, which would have been necessary had the curving tracks into Plumstead Road been of a more conventional radius. As it was, both the Ordnance Arms on the left and the Royal Mortar Hotel (out of shot on the right) retained their structural integrity. B.T.Cooke

Left The date is 26th April 1952, and Abbey Wood Depot is being reconstructed for buses. In creating this new entrance to the depot, the builders have laid three temporary tram tracks which can be easily removed after 5th July. J.H.Meredith

Below Car 165 has an Alpax windscreen at the end facing the camera and a Charlton wooden one surrounding the opposite platform. The tram is viewed leaving Well Hall Road at the junction with Shooters Hill Road. This section between Woolwich and Eltham was opened on 23rd July 1910, and witnessed some of the heaviest passenger traffic of the First World War. Four wheel M class cars pulling trailers had the task of ferrying thousands of Arsenal workers to and from makeshift camps adjacent to tram route 44. At the end of the tramway era things were a little more civilised, but passenger loadings were still high, because routes 44 and 46 served a 'natural' traffic corridor. D.A.Thompson

car ground over pennies placed on the line at such strategic locations as Westminster Bridge and the Victoria Embankment.

Stage 8 of the conversion programme saw routes 36/38, 40, 44, 46 and 72 replaced by bus services 177, 163, 182 and 186. A total of 162 trams was supplanted by 117 buses, a fact which reflected the belief that there was overcapacity in these last six tram routes.

The authorities were out in force on the last day, and LT inspectors tried their best to guide the flow of humanity on to each overloaded tramcar. Many folk refused to get off at the London termini, and at least one group of determined travellers clocked up three round trips on the same 46 from Beresford Square to Southwark Bridge. For those who wanted to pay five shillings for the privilege, the LRTL hired two trams for a farewell tour. The trip was oversubscribed, but unfortunately LT could only spare cars 1931 and 1908, which were designated A and B respectively. The tour began at Southwark Bridge whence the two trams departed at 2.30pm. The procession then headed for the Old Kent Road and Greenwich Church. There the convoy reversed to return via New Cross Gate, Westminster Bridge Road and

Left Car 302 is about to reverse at Lee Green. There was an overlap of overhead wires from Lee Green change pit outside the fire station to the bridge over the Quaggy in Lee High Road. This crossover could therefore be used by conduit and overhead trolley trams. R. Hubble

Below The Millennium celebrations have focussed attention on the Greenwich Observatory and its contribution to world time keeping. Car 1867 is pictured in Lee High Road, almost exactly on the line of zero longitude, the Prime Meridian. D.A. Thompson

Addington Street siding. Here there occurred some tram shunting to the accompaniment of the clicking of many camera shutters. Off the party went again via the Embankment, St George's Circus, the Elephant and Castle, New Cross, Lewisham, Lee Green change pit and Westhorne Avenue, Eltham, where a large group photo was organised. The trams then reversed and made for Eltham Church, Well Hall Road, Woolwich Common and Beresford Square. Here they crossed on to Plumstead Road for the journey to Abbey Wood. After the party had alighted from cars 1931 and 1908 to partake of their tea break, the two trams were driven to the Abbey Wood Depot approach track. The return to central London took in Penhall Road and Charlton Works. Other specials on the rails were two cars for the Ian Allan Bus Spotters Club, Car 1946 for the Omnibus Society, and Car 1988 which was hired by the Infantile Paralysis Fellowship. Passengers on this vehicle were kitted out in Edwardian dress and the decorated tram was accompanied by a vintage motor car.

Late in the evening of 5th July, the last special trams made their way through crowd thronged streets. Car 1952 transported local VIPs and the mayors of nine London boroughs from Charlton Works to New Cross Depot, and the official last tram, Car 1951, left Woolwich at 12.10am and arrived at New Cross at around 1.15am on 6th July. Driver Albert Fuller and Conductor William Bedford were the pair chosen for the ceremonial last ride. However, when the car entered the depot yard, John Cliff, Deputy Chairman of London Transport, was at the helm. He had been specially issued with Metropolitan Stage Carriage badge T 15000 for the occasion. Lord Latham, London Transport Executive Chairman, then greeted his deputy, made a short speech and finally saw the official last car home amidst scenes of great excitement – fireworks, flares, communal singing and blaring of car horns filled the night. Someone even managed to get on the roof of Car 1951, where he patriotically waved the Union Jack until the forces of law and order persuaded him to come down! During the evening, many trams due into the depot for the last time were merely reversed outside and sent on their way to Penhall Road. The last 46 to reach New Cross Gate was Car 187 which arrived at 1.35am; this was the final vehicle to use Lee Green change pit.

As far as can be ascertained, the last 44 from Eltham and the last tram to traverse the Beresford Square curve into Beresford Street was Car 559. On board was John Wills and a friend who were then turfed off by the conductor as the tram continued empty to Penhall Road. Another observer at Beresford

Above The battle to lay tram tracks over Westminster Bridge had been a protracted and acrimonious one. The LCC succeeded in getting its tramcars across the River Thames, but then failed to secure through routes in the City of Westminster and West End. The battles of the first decade of the Twentieth Century seem an age away as a nearly empty car on route 40 is pictured in the last few days of operation on Westminster Bridge.

Below Posters describing 'The Fruits of Tram Scrapping' adorn Car 1931, a special hired by LRTL for the last day. The tone of the messages chalked on the tram reflects the sympathies of what London Transport would have termed a minority interest group. The location is the Marquis of Granby road junction, New Cross.

Above The last night celebrations on the Victoria Embankment were preserved in the memory of many by the possession of bent and distorted pennies placed on the tram rails. Aside from the defacers of coins of the realm, other merrymakers seem just intent on enjoying the atmosphere. Most people had by now given up any hope of one last ride and were just there to help along the party.

Right Car 1951 briefly becomes a triple decker as it enters New Cross Depot for the final official farewell in front of the London Transport grandees. Luckily the patriotic gathering on the roof was later persuaded to vacate their vantage spot before the tram could be driven to Penhall Road. The Metropolitan Police have also turned out in some numbers, but their presence was largely symbolic, as the celebrations were generally good natured.

Square, and later at Abbey Wood and Penhall Road, was Alan Jackson, and it is from his account that we can determine an accurate summary of the last car movements. Car 337 was the last 46 to leave from Southwark Bridge, whilst sister Car 309 left the Embankment at 11.40 on the final through trip to Abbey Wood. Car 309 was later spotted by Mr Jackson at Abbey Wood where it left empty for Penhall Road at 1.05am. Half an hour previously at Abbey Wood, Car 340 had almost been ravaged by souvenir hunters until the police intervened, thoughtfully supplying a uniformed officer to stand on the front platform as it made its last journey to the scrapyard. After Car 309 had departed, this left only Car 592 in Abbey Wood Depot. The tram had developed a fault and would be dispatched as soon as repairs could be effected.

Alan Jackson then cycled to Penhall Road, arriving at 1.35am. Here, amongst the crowds of well wishers and somewhat inebri-ated revellers, a few dedicated tramway enthusiasts observed the final car movements. At 2.01am cars 187 and 1858 arrived from New Cross, to be followed at 2.27am by Car 592 which had finally made it from Abbey Wood. In so doing, it had become the last London tram to use the Woolwich change pit. The tram ran as far as Church Lane crossover, reversed and entered Penhall Road at 2.35am. There was then a wait of almost an hour before the arrival of cars 1946, 1912, 1951, 1995, 1863, 1952, 1909, 1988 and finally Car 1931. Some of this batch had been delayed in the confines of New Cross Depot, waiting for a crew from the British Transport Commission to complete the day's filming of *The Elephant Will Never Forget*. Car 1931 entered Penhall Road at 3.35am.

Below Car 337, chalked up as the Eltham Flier, brings to an end the tramway era on Southwark Bridge, as the final southbound 46. LT Museum

Above The last night was certainly not an occasion for tram enthusiasts to celebrate, but Car 2, somewhat surprisingly, has survived to the end, and is seen here outside New Cross Depot on its last service run. G.F.Ashwell

AFTERMATH

THE JULY 1952 issue of *London Transport Magazine* was devoted mainly to articles describing the passing of the trams. In a message from the Chairman, Lord Latham sums up, what to him, were the main features of the conversion. He concludes by stating that 'the final replacement of the trams by a more modern, more flexible and more manoeuvrable vehicle will be a landmark in the history of the capital which we serve, and a major work of civic importance'. The validity of these opinions was shared by the whole team assembled by London Transport to complete the task. Mr J. B. Burnell, Operating Manager (Central Road Services), seems to echo the tone in a piece entitled *Zero Hour Was Exciting*, where he concentrates on the training of over 1,900 motormen to drive diesel buses. The Chief Mechanical Engineer (Road Services), also chimes in with his tale, headed *Engineers Had Problems To Solve*, which tells of the trials and tribulations of converting tram depots into bus garages. In short, everyone

appeared to be mightily satisfied with the outcome. *The Observer* of 6th July, called the last tram process 'one of London Transport's most inspired pieces of public relations'. The *News of the World* cried triumphantly in a headline: *London's Traffic Will Speed Up As The Last Tram Goes Home*. No dissenting

voices, other than those of tramway enthusiasts, were raised to question the logic of the programme. Everyone (at least at 55 Broadway) seemed to envisage a rosy future for Central Road Services.

Away from newspaper headlines, the travelling public in the morning peak of Monday

Top The dismal spectacle of a full Penhall Road scrapyard is etched against the backdrop of the mounds and former gravel workings of Charlton Heights. These regimented rows of doomed vehicles would gradually be whittled down to just one tram – Car 179, which was scrapped on 29th January 1953. R.Hubble

Right Track removal is proceeding apace in Woolwich Road as the former staff 'offices' await their turn to join the bonfire. R.Hubble

7th July began to accustom themselves to the new situation, and soon the memory of the trams faded. Some months after the conversion, the final tally for the programme was stated to be 745 trams and 10 trolleybuses replaced by 824 buses.

The honeymoon lasted just over one month. On 26th August a London evening newspaper reported:

'London's street congestion has been made more acute by the passing of the trams and the consequent increase in the number of buses. Station approaches are becoming very popular as parking places in the suburbs and another problem is being set up by all day parking in suburban side roads. Motorists are finding that continuous traffic jams and "crawling" put up their rate of petrol consumption and cause mechanical faults through overheating.'

This piece served to highlight some of the potential problems which would eventually nullify the tram scrappers' claims that the average traffic speed along former tram routes would increase significantly. Although it would have been fair to point out that the ending of petrol rationing was a major factor in the increase of private motoring, the warning signs for the future were already apparent.

Throughout the rest of 1952 and into 1953, the work of dismantling and removing the remains of track and tramcars continued. The staff at Penhall Road continued to dismember the fleet and on 29th January 1953, E/3 Car 179 had the dubious honour of being the last London tram to be scrapped. Apart from the Felthams and LCC Car 1 sold to Leeds, no other cars had been sold for further service elsewhere, but London Transport did manage to sell the trucks from 10 HR/2 cars and the equipments from 80 E/3s to Alexandria in Egypt.

Some idea of the atmosphere at Penhall Road can be gleaned from this account by Fr Benedict Sankey:

My final tramway experience in London was in October 1952, at the start of my final year at Cambridge. I took the bus to Penhall Road – noticing en route a tram at the CRD – it had a 72 number stencil, and I now know it was Car 1858. I had a look at what was going on in Penhall Road yard, and got into conversation with a friendly official. He was an ex-MET man and had no doubts about the superiority of the trams! He took me inside the fence and on board an ex-East Ham or West Ham car – with that dreadful varnished woodwork in alternate dark and light planks, as the E/1s once had. Somebody had sawed away the window uprights from one of the stairhead partitions, and my guide commented on the soundness of the timber. Then he gave me a lesson in driving – unfortunately only stationary! – and finally took me aboard a snowbroom. This had much

Fire consumes Car 179 and the last of the working tram fleet is no more. This car had spent most of its working life on the Kingsway Subway services.

'What goes down must come up!' is the caption suggested by the photographer. The date is 8th October 1952, and the location is Tooting Broadway.
A.B.Cross

pleasanter interior woodwork, familiar to me because I had encountered ex-London B class trams in Southampton. Even after years as a works car the interior was quite prepossessing! I'd like to think it was 022, but I just don't know. It was a good, if melancholy, farewell to London's trams . . . the final words lie with my guide at Penhall Road who remarked: They're taking them off, they'll have to put them back . . .

Snowbroom 022 was eventually retrieved and after many years out of sight of the public was restored by the efforts of the LCC Tramways Trust. It was reconstructed in its original guise as open top B class Car 106, and now runs in the company of E/1 Car 1622, another LCCTT masterpiece of restoration, at the National Tramway Museum.

On the roads formerly served by trams the track removal gangs had been making haste and by the end of 1953 most of the rails had been lifted. An interesting view of immediate post tramway South London can be experienced by watching the 1953 British film classic *Genevieve*, which featured the London to Brighton veteran car run. Some scenes depict conduit tracks, and tram rails on the County Hall roundabout play a crucial role in the film's happy end! Not such a pleasant outcome awaited three men caught stealing three tons of tram rails, worth £10, from Blackfriars Road. At Tower Bridge Magistrates Court one was fined £30, and the others £10 each.

In the months following final abandonment very little track was left in situ. The most notable section of permanent way to remain intact was the complete layout at Beresford Square which outlived the demise of the local trolleybuses in 1959, and was finally covered in the 1980s, when much of the area was bypassed by a new dual carriageway road. Ironically, in other areas of London there was still some track left from pre-war conversions, and well into the 1960s rails could be seen in the road surface at places as far apart as Twickenham, Edmonton and Barking.

Some conduit cable ducts were retained for the LT private telephone network and, where appropriate, some lengths of conduit track were buried under the road surface as a means of strengthening the whole highway. A case in point was at the Vauxhall giratory system, where approach road alterations several decades after final abandonment of the trams resulted in the unearthing of many conduit yokes. Other direct evidence of the trams was preserved in the shape of rectangular manhole covers in pavements which gave access to cable runs. These relics of the past were often embossed with the legend London County Council Tramways, and outside the old county boundary covers bearing the words Croydon Corporation Tramways could be observed on the pavements adjacent to the former local tram services.

The overhead wire equipped routes were dismantled quickly and some traction standards which doubled as street lamps were retained by local authorities, but many of these had a short life and by the mid 1950s they had been supplanted by various designs of concrete lamp post. At some locations the rails were lifted before the overhead was removed. Woolwich Borough Council was in such a hurry to improve the junction of Well Hall Road and Eltham High Street that the tramlines disappeared in a few days, leaving the apparently serviceable overhead wires hanging rather forlornly over the scene.

Granite setts and woodblocks were extracated from the highway by the ton and, as John Chambers remembers, some were put to good use:

Our family moved from Forest Hill to Bromley Road, Catford in November 1953, by which time of course the trams and their tracks had gone. However, I do recall gangs of workmen lifting hatches in the pavement to remove the copper cables which I guess were part of the power supply, and chop them up with axes into short lengths for easy removal. After that the only direct evidence of the trams were one or two metal point box covers in the pavement. An indirect piece of evidence was the construction by my father of a terrace in our back garden using granite setts which had been lifted from the streets when the tram tracks were removed.

However, even after the physical remains of the tramways had disappeared, the doubts about the wisdom of the conversion began to take root. In the *Kentish Independent* of 16th October 1953, the following short piece appeared: 'Every day more and more tons of London's disused and rusty tram tracks are uprooted. Cyclists, drivers and pedestrians are pleased to see them go, but many road safety officials do not share their delight. For, contrary to what was expected, there has not been a big decline in the number of road accidents since the removal of the tracks started. Take for example, the boroughs of Woolwich and Greenwich, where "Operation Dig Up" is nearly complete. From January to August 1952 – when the tracks were down – there were 432 accidents in Woolwich. For the corresponding period

A section of track which survived to be classified as a part of metropolitan industrial archaeology was situated next to Queen's Road Station, Peckham. These rails and passing loops led to the depot and stables of the London Tramways Company, whose horse tramway between New Cross Gate and Camberwell Green was opened on 29th January 1872. J.H.Meredith

this year accident figures rose by 37 to 469. At Greenwich too, more people were injured (89 more) during the same period. Road Safety Organiser for Greenwich, Mr H. A. Fellows, is convinced that the increase in the borough is due to the disappearance of the tracks, and more especially the trams. – 'They might have rumbled and rattled a bit, but the dear old trams certainly kept the number of accidents down – he said.'

Well, this wasn't quite the outcome the planners had predicted, and further rumbles of discontent surfaced in a South London Press article on 21st July 1953:

'It is now about a year since the last tram left South London, and that is perhaps a reasonable period in which to judge whether the change to buses has brought the anticipated relief to traffic and passengers. No comment comes from the great majority of people so long as they get to and from home with no great hitch or discomfort. It is when something goes wrong, and the victims of an unusually long queue at the stop get home full of grievance, that the cry is heard: Why did they ever scrap the trams?

'The silence of motorists is more significant. These were the road users who used to complain about the hold ups by the juggernauts of the streets. There are still traffic jams, varying from the normal to the sensational (as at the Coronation), but it is hard to single out any one class of vehicle as guilty of creating the nuisance. A reader, C. B.

Smith, has argued very reasonably that, for a scheme costing £9 million, the improvement is not impressive. Queues are not shorter, and fares continue to rise. Buses still cause confusion on the Victoria Embankment and – this is a newer objection – buses are held up by fog and snow far more than trams ever were. He is supported by another correspondent who has a newer complaint: pollution of the air by the fumes of diesel engined buses.'

Even as late as April 1955, a group of six South London borough councils were still pressing for better transport facilities for the area, plus of course the extension of the tube to Camberwell. The whole debate was covered by the *Evening News* under the headline *Oh for the days of the old trams!*

Other remnants of the tramway past were a number of green painted section boxes; some of these were used by London Transport to store equipment, particularly spare ticket machines for use in emergency. The section boxes were gradually removed by local authorities in the 1960s as part of a campaign to clear up some of the clutter of

The vista from the Royal Greenwich Observatory to the River Thames in 1999 included the tramways power station with its four chimneys. Behind the former LCC building one can see the Millennium Dome.

outdated street furniture. Certainly, the author recalls two such boxes, one outside a parade of shops in Lee High Road, near Glenton Road, and another more prominent example at the southern end of Westhorne Avenue by Eltham Green. The Westhorne Avenue example was topped by a smaller box which contained a departmental telephone, it was listed in the official timetable for LT employees under the number OT100 – another LT phone was situated a few yards away at the inspectors' shelter opposite the Yorkshire Grey crossover (terminus of route 44).

Former tram depots were now fulfilling their roles as bus garages, and so extensive was the rebuilding programme that it was difficult to imagine they were ever used for electric traction. Norwood Depot building survived as a silent memorial to past glories. It was an eerie place when, on 30th October 1953, John Price met up with the watchman who previously had 34 years service at Brixton change pit. Some of his reminiscences were transcribed by John Price:

There was a very small conductor at Norwood Depot called Cook, who would use his ticket rack to ring the bell. The Norwood men have now all gone to Stockwell Bus Garage. Some are now at Elmers End. One or two who didn't pass for bus driving are now on bus washing, at New Cross and Stockwell. Being a tram man is a bar to promotion now. Forty men at one exam included 26 tram men, mostly from Telford Avenue, but of 14 chosen, only one was a tram man.

These remarks may be accurate, but some of the conclusions are debatable. One thing is for certain, they betray some personal bitterness towards London Transport. One can sympathise with an ex-motorman having to earn a living washing buses!

Hampstead Depot in Cressy Road appeared in the accounts of the British Transport Commission for 1953. It was proposed to use it as a garage for British Road Services, which was the state run road haulage organisation.

The most interesting structure, born of the tramway age and now disused, was the Kingsway Subway. During the Coronation celebrations of 1953 it was used for storing buses, but afterwards it was disused and seemingly forgotten until early 1955 when Lord Lucas of Chilworth asked the govern-

ment in the House of Lords to consider using the tunnel as a one way street for road traffic. Lord Hawke replied that in 1952 it was calculated that such a scheme would cost £1,200,000, and that the expense was out of proportion to the benefit. Not unsurprisingly, the politicians changed their minds, and in November 1963 part of the tunnel from a new entrance on Waterloo Bridge to a ramp just north of the old Aldwych Tram Station site, was opened for northbound traffic. The whole course of the subway was not sacrificed to the internal combustion engine and students of history can still marvel at the northern ramp, where conduit tracks rise to meet Southampton Row. It is an impressive sight, and a fitting monument to the LCC's imaginative transport policy The largest edifice to the past glories of the tramcar is the former LCC Tramways power station at Greenwich. This building with its four chimneys straddles the famous line of longitude – the Greenwich Meridian. Just over 300 workers were once employed there to supply electricity to the post-war network. At the end of the Twentieth Century, the building still occupied a prominent position on the Thames waterfront, easily spotted from the vantage point in Greenwich Park next to the Royal Observatory.

HOME FOR A TRAM

ON hearing some time ago that the L.T.E. were planning to preserve two London trams in their museum, I was disappointed to discover that both cars were of 1907-1910 vintage, and that they were to be kept at Reigate—well out of the London area. I have therefore obtained a quotation from the L.T.E. for one of their more modern cars, with a view to purchasing it as a "museum piece." Unfortunately, it seems unlikely that the L.T.E will be able to accommodate the car, and I would be pleased to know if any of your readers who might be interested in the scheme know of a suitable site—preferably covered to protect the car from the weather—in the London area where such a car could be kept on view.—*P. J. Davis, East Dulwich-grove, Dulwich, S.E.22.*

The London trams which did escape from Penhall Road to Leeds only had a limited career in the Yorkshire city. A political change in the make up of Leeds City Council was to signify a different attitude to the local tramways, and by November 1959 they were no more. Most of the ex-London Felthams perished, but former LCC Car 1 was returned to her native soil. She had entered service in Leeds on 1st December 1951 and was finally withdrawn in September 1957 to be presented to the British Transport Commission as an exhibit for the proposed Museum of British Transport. Car 1 arrived back at Charlton Works on 28th November 1957. It was later joined by Car 2099, which was restored as MET Car 355. Unfortunately, the BTC museum on the site of the former Clapham Depot was subject to political pressures of its own and it was closed down in the early 1970s. Car 1 was transferred to the National Tramway Museum, where it has languished for some years as a non-working exhibit. Feltham Car 355 eventually found a home at the London Transport Museum, Covent Garden, where it shares the billing with Car 1025 and West Ham Car 290. Another Feltham to survive was Car 2085 which was shipped to the Seashore Trolley Museum in Maine, USA; like Car 1, it is not in serviceable condition. One tram that is preserved in an operational state is HR/2 Car 1858, which was saved from the scrapyard by the efforts of P. J. Davis. It eventually moved on from Chess-ington to a permanent home at the East Anglia Transport Museum, Carlton Colville near Lowestoft.

Electric traction, in the form of the trolleybuses, finally disappeared from the streets of London in May 1962; the whole of Central Road Services was now centred on the diesel bus. Thus it remained for over three decades – three decades of new highways, growing congestion, traffic pollution and loss of passengers. The situation cried out for an influential group of planners and politicians who had the courage and vision to break the vicious circle of urban gridlock. Much to their credit, the officials in charge of London Transport eventually conceived a new tramway system centred on the Borough of Croydon. If the descendants of the 1927 wellwishers at East Croydon Station were to return today they would witness a fine, new tramway facility in the shape of Croydon Tramlink. But that, as they say, is another story!

Leeds Car 301, ex-LT Car 1, looks extremely smart in its new dark red livery. Unfortunately its passenger carrying days in the Yorkshire city were numbered, but on the credit side it was later rescued for preservation. *S.E.Letts*

Three prominent tramway photographers were asked to submit their favourite London views of the postwar era. Each caption is in the words of the creator of the photograph.

PHOTOGRAPHIC RETROSPECTIVE

J.H. MEREDITH *Above* 'Apart from portraying London's finest tram (Car 1), this view recalls a most enjoyable SCTS tour, driven by Chief Inspector Perry (to the left of the tram). It also shows the imposing entrance arch to Blackwall Tunnel – like the trams, another great civic enterprise – with one of the specially designed Tunnel STLs about to descend on the 108 Crystal Palace to Bromley-by-Bow route. In every way, the indication on the tram **EXTRA SPECIAL** fits the occasion.'

C. CARTER *Below* 'Favourite view – most people will surely find this a bit difficult. We all have so many favourite views! However, I will settle for Car 340 on the Embankment at 5pm, 5th July 1952. This was the last car on which I rode. I had come on it from New Cross, and I dashed over the road while people were alighting. Camera at the ready, I just got the shot as the car started to move. Every seat was occupied, as you can see.'

A.B. CROSS *Facing page* 'Reflections on the Past – A very heavy spring shower left the road and tram track awash to give a classic example of photographer's luck. Car 394 arrived from Thornton Heath just as the sun came out, making it possible to capture the puddles, the spray from the trucks of the moving car and the reflections on the shiny road – all in 1/50th of a second. Definitely one of my favourite photographs. South End, Croydon, 7th April 1951, the last day of tramway operation in Croydon.'

A further three pictures, but this time taken by men sadly no longer with us, who spent their life with tramways and can still display their talents through their photographic legacies.

D.A.THOMPSON

Facing page top No photographic section on London's tramways would be complete without a tribute to the work of the late Don Thompson. All the elements of Don's finely crafted approach come into play in this view of Highbury Corner. Bright sunshine illuminates a street tableau of post-war London life – the people and the tramcar contribute to a memorable scene.

R.ELLIOTT

Facing page bottom Richard Elliott's shot of Car 1385 in the back streets of Woolwich is another evocative view of a bygone age. Richard was employed at Charlton Works, and often broke his journey home to Abbey Wood to observe and photograph the tramway scene. One can visualise the bright red and cream paintwork of Car 1385, which is in stark contrast to the seedy, rather run down, nature of the shops and tenements.

R.HUBBLE

Above The late Roy Hubble's "perfect" tramway vista was probably something akin to the shot he took of this line up in Well Hall Road. This is one of those fortuitous events, where the photographer just happens to be at the right place, at the right time. From the rear we have: an HR2, E3 Car 2002, ex-East Ham Car 95 and ex-West Ham Car 309. What's more, the sun is shining over Eltham!

APPENDIX

MAP

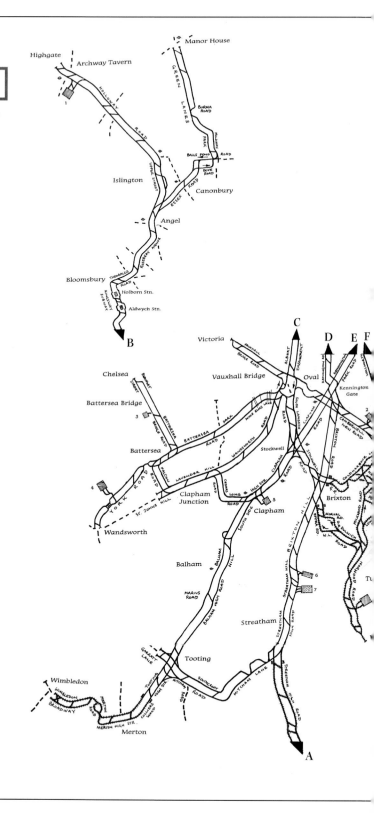

Key

Tramway – conduit equipped

Tramway – overhead wire equipped

Change Pit – trolley to conduit

Interlaced Track

Tube Station

Scale – excluding junction layouts and distances between double tracks –

One Mile   One Kilometre

List of Streets

S.B.R.	Southwark Bridge Road
L.S.	Lancaster Street
C.S.	Church Street
N.R.	Nelson Road
R.R.	Romney Road
T.R.	Trafalgar Road
B.S.	Beresford Street
G.E.	Greens End
K.H.	Knee Hill
W.R.	Wanless Road
W.L.	Water Lane
G.R.	Gresham Road
D.R.	Dalberg Road

List of Depots and Yards

1. Holloway Depot
2. Camberwell Depot
3. Battersea PW Yard
4. Wandsworth Depot
5. Clapham Depot
6. Brixton Hill Depot
7. Streatham, Telford Avenue Depot
8. Norwood Depot
9. New Cross Depot
10. Deptford PW Yard
11. Charlton Works
12. Penhall Scrap Yard
13. Abbey Wood Depot
14. Thornton Heath Depot
15. Purley Depot

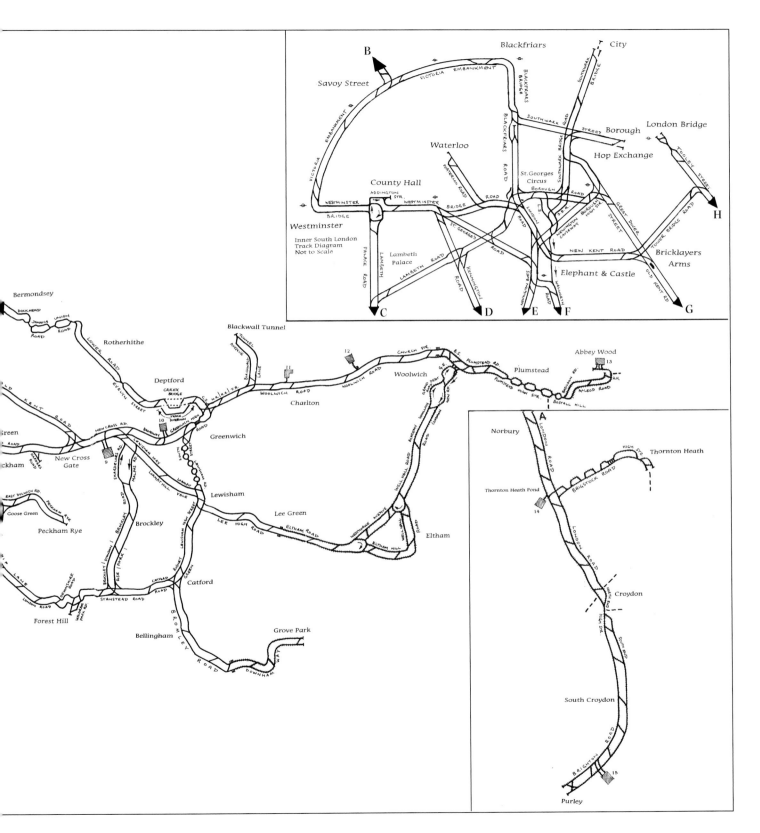

APPENDIX

TRAM ROUTES IN 1950

No.	Route
2	Wimbledon and Victoria Embankment (via Westminster Bridge)
4	Wimbledon and Victoria Embankment (via Blackfriars Bridge)
6	Tooting and City (Southwark Bridge)
8	Victoria Station and Victoria Station (via Clapham and Streatham)
10	Tooting Broadway and City (Southwark)
12	Wandsworth High Street and London Bridge (Borough)
16	Purley and Victoria Embankment (via Westminster Bridge)
18	Purley and Victoria Embankment (via Blackfriars Bridge)
20	Victoria Station and Victoria Station (via Streatham and Clapham)
22	Tooting Broadway and Victoria Embankment (via Balham and Clapham)
24	Tooting Broadway and Victoria Embankment (via Streatham and Brixton)
26	Clapham Junction and London Bridge (Borough)
28	Clapham Junction and Victoria Station
31	Wandsworth High Street and Islington Green
33	West Norwood and Manor House Station
34	Chelsea (Kings Road), Camberwell Green and Blackfriars
35	Highgate (Archway Tavern) and Forest Hill
36	Abbey Wood and Victoria Embankment (via Blackfriars Bridge)
38	Abbey Wood and Victoria Embankment (via Westminster Bridge)
40	Plumstead (Wickham Lane). Woolwich and Victoria Embankment (Savoy Street)
42	Croydon (Coombe Road) and Thornton Heath
44	Woolwich (Beresford Square) and Eltham (Middle Park Avenue)
46	Woolwich (Beresford Square), New Cross and City (Southwark)
48	West Norwood, Elephant & Castle and City (Southwark)
52	Grove Park Station and City (Southwark)
54	Grove Park Station and Victoria Station
56	Peckham Rye and Victoria Embankment (via Westminster Bridge)
58	Blackwall Tunnel, Forest Hill and Victoria Station
60	Dulwich Library and City (Southwark)
62	Lewisham, Forest Hill and Victoria Embankment (Savoy Street) (via Westminster Bridge)
66	Forest Hill and Victoria Station
68	Greenwich Church and Waterloo Station
70	Greenwich Church, Bermondsey and London Bridge Station
72	Woolwich (Beresford Square), New Cross and Victoria Embankment (Savoy Street) (via Westminster Bridge)
74	Grove Park Station, Downham (Bromley Road) and Blackfriars
78	West Norwood and Victoria Station
84	Peckham Rye and Victoria Embankment (via Blackfriars Bridge)

This sign belongs to the once-standard black and white Ministry of Transport range, which were topped with a red warning triangle. This particular example once stood on the southern approach to Blackfriars Bridge, where the trams swung from the centre to the side of the carriageway. Ironically this photograph was taken on 6th July 1952, some hours after the trams had indeed been 'pinched' by London Transport!

ALL-NIGHT TRAM ROUTES

No.	Route
1	Streatham Library and Victoria Embankment (via Tooting, Balham, Clapham, Blackfriars Bridge and Westminster)
1	Tooting Broadway and Victoria Embankment (via Streatham, Brixton, Kennington, Westminster Bridge and Blackfriars)
3	Battersea (Princes Head) and Blackfriars
5	Downham (Bromley Road) and Victoria Embankment (Savoy Street)
7	New Cross Gate and Victoria Embankment (Savoy Street)
26	Clapham Junction, Westminster Station and London Bridge (Borough)
35	Highgate (Archway Tavern), Bloomsbury and Westminster

APPENDIX

FLEET ALLOCATION – 1st January 1950

This list has been compiled with the help of John Barrie and John Wills, and represents the state of research at the time of writing. It is possible that certain trams have been wrongly allocated – this may be due to incorrect 'spotting' of car numbers, typing errors on behalf of London Transport clerks or mistakes in transferring written records. The author tenders his apologies for any incorrect information. Obviously many cars, particularly E/3s, HR/2s with trolleys and the 1930 series E/1s, were moved from depot to depot after 1950, and a sizeable number ended up at either New Cross or Abbey Wood.

After each depot name **the figures in heavy print indicate tram routes** and *those in italics show the number of trams allocated to that route*. Routes marked EX indicate extra vehicles used at peak hours, or for short workings.

Abbey Wood.
36/38:*26*, **44**(weekdays):*10*, **46**:*20*, **46EX**:*3*.
81–100, 295–302, 304–312, 331–334, 344, 1137, 1142, 1143, 1172, 1225, 1230, 1231, 1361–1363, 1378, 1407, 1409, 1478.

Camberwell – later renamed Walworth Garage.
34:*29*, **35**:*21*, **56/84**:*20*, **58**:*37*, **60**(weekdays):*9*, **62**(weekdays):*14*.
101–111, 113–122, 126–128, 132–147, 149–159, 161–164, 167, 172, 174, 177, 181, 188–194, 577, 592, 593, 598, 1103, 1372, 1375, 1377, 1380, 1381, 1384, 1385, 1395–1397, 1854–1864, 1866–1880, 1882, 1884, 1885, 1887, 1888, 1890–1897, 1931, 1933–1935, 1968–1971, 1974, 1977, 1979–1981, 1984, 1986–1988.

Clapham.
2/4:*32*, **6**(weekdays):*9*, **8/20**:*8*, **22/24**(weekdays):*15*, **26**:*12*, **28**:*12*, **1**:*3*.
1312, 1571, 1573, 1581, 1582, 1589, 1592–1595, 1597, 1669, 1671, 1672, 1674, 1675, 1727, 1730, 1743, 1744, 1758, 1763, 1764, 1768–1772, 1775, 1777–1779, 1781–1785, 1787, 1790, 1791, 1793–1799, 1801–1806, 1809–1815, 1817–1820, 1822–1824, 1826–1830, 1832–1834, 1836–1841, 1843–1851.

Holloway – later renamed Highgate Depot.
31:*6*, **33**:*5*, **35**:*8*, **night 35**:*1*. *Holloway also housed 150 trolleybuses.*
168–171, 173, 175, 176, 178–180, 182–187, 1943–1949.

New Cross.
36/38:*43*, **40**:*33*, **46**:*22*, **52**(weekdays):*19*, **54**:*43*, **66**(weekdays):*16*, **68**:*19*, **70**:*11*, **72**:*21*, **72EX**(weekdays):*8*, **74**:*27*, **5**:*3*, **7**:*2*.
160, 335–343, 552–568, 570–575, 578–582, 584–591, 595, 596, 599–601, 802, 836, 839, 840, 916, 936, 940, 947, 948, 953, 960, 961, 978, 981, 982, 984, 985, 993–996, 1003, 1005, 1007, 1009, 1017, 1019, 1022, 1024, 1025, 1030, 1032, 1033, 1038, 1042, 1049, 1083, 1087–1090, 1092, 1094, 1128, 1144, 1145, 1163, 1170, 1171, 1173–1175, 1177, 1182, 1190, 1191, 1195, 1204, 1208, 1211–1213, 1215, 1216, 1218–1220, 1223, 1226, 1227, 1233, 1244, 1246–1248, 1250–1252, 1255, 1260, 1267, 1270, 1273, 1275, 1291, 1310, 1316, 1317, 1350, 1355, 1358, 1367, 1382, 1390, 1406, 1408, 1410, 1413–1415, 1419, 1423, 1444, 1480, 1481, 1485–1489, 1491, 1493, 1494, 1496, 1498, 1499, 1501, 1503, 1504, 1508, 1520, 1525, 1527, 1529–1534, 1537, 1538, 1540–1542, 1544–1549, 1553, 1555, 1557, 1561–1570, 1574, 1576, 1577, 1579, 1587, 1588, 1590, 1598, 1599, 1601–1604, 1606, 1608, 1610, 1612–1614, 1617–1619, 1621, 1624, 1626–1631, 1636, 1638, 1640, 1642–1648, 1650–1655, 1657–1665, 1667, 1670, 1673, 1676, 1923, 1924, 2042, 2043, 2045–2050.

Norwood.
10(weekdays):*19*, **16/18**:*9*, **16/18EX**:*12*, **33**:*18*, **48**:*10*, **78**:*11*.
2, 165, 166, 1352, 1353, 1357, 1359, 1365, 1366, 1368, 1369, 1386–1388, 1391–1393, 1398–1402, 1422, 1492, 1500, 1502, 1506, 1507, 1514, 1913–1922, 1929, 1930, 1932, 1936–1942, 1956, 1966, 1989–2003.

Purley.
16/18:*10*, **16/18EX**:*5*, **42**:*13*.
375, 377–395, 397–399, 1904–1912.

Streatham – Brixton Hill.
8/20:*5*, **16/18**:*11*, **16/18EX**:*22*, **22/24**(weekdays):*7*

Streatham – Telford Avenue
– later renamed Brixton Garage.
8/20:*16*, **10**(weekdays):*2*, **16/18**:*10*, **22/24**(weekdays):*8*, **1**:*3*.
1, 2052–2061, 2066, 2068–2090, 2092–2098, 2100–2108, 2110–2112, 2114–2121, 2123–2129, 2131–2162, 2164.

Wandsworth.
12:*16*, **26**:*7*, **night 26**:*1*, **31**:*12*, **3**:*1*.
Wandsworth also supplied 21 trolleybuses for route **612**.
195–210, 1761, 1762, 1766, 1773, 1925–1928, 1950–1955, 1957–1965.

Charlton Works Staff Cars.
326 – July 1947 to April 1951
327 – July 1947 to April 1951
330 – July 1947 to April 1951
1388 – Jan 1951 to April 1951
1392 – April 1951 to Oct 1951
1409 – April 1951 to May 1951
1664 – April 1951 to Jan 1952
1400 – April 1951 to Sept 1951
1493 – Sept 1951 to Dec 1951
1804 – Oct 1951 to Jan 1952
1798 – Dec 1951 to Jan 1952
2056 – Jan 1952 to April 1952
2055 – Jan 1952 to July 1952

TRAM STOPS

Electric tramways in Great Britain were equipped with fixed stopping places, either of the request or compulsory type.

In 1933 the London Passenger Transport Board inherited a mixture of stop sign sizes and designs, all of which proclaimed a message on the CARS STOP HERE theme.

At many locations on the post-war tram system the public could be forgiven for thinking that the London Transport 'house style' had passed them by, because many ex-LCC stop signs survived until almost the end of the trams. It remains a mystery why action was not taken to standardise all tram 'flags', but one must consider that the men from 55 Broadway were reluctant to spend any extra money on the 'doomed' tramways.

LCC STYLE This is a classic example of an LCC cloverleaf request stop, which has been fixed to an iron column and pedestal. It is situated in London Road, Elephant and Castle. It features white lettering on a red background, and the word STOP has been applied in blue on a white background. J.C.Gillham

LCC STYLE An LCC cloverleaf compulsory stop once stood at the corner of Powis Street and Green's End, Woolwich. Services 44, 46 and 72, which terminated a few yards further on in Beresford Square, used this as a head stop, with most of the disembarking passengers making a beeline for the shops in Powis Street. J.C.Gillham

In the shadow of one of the railway bridges at Loughborough Junction is this brown and white LCC fare stage sign. The date is 6th January 1951. J.C.Gillham

An LCC vertical type request stop stands next to Kennington Road by Lambeth North Station. Even on 28th June 1952, when this view was taken, one can still detect evidence of the wartime white bands, painted during the blackout as an aid to pedestrians and road users. J.C.Gillham

In Peckham High Road by Sumner Avenue we observe Car 1859, with its LAST TRAM WEEK poster, as it passes an LCC horizontal type request stop which has been attached to a plain steel pole. J.C.Gillham

This style is based on the former London United and Metropolitan Electric stops. TRAMS STOP HERE is depicted in black on a cream background. The word TRAMWAYS is in white letters on a blue bar, with a red roundel above and below. The sign is attached to a concrete post. The location is Great Dover Street by Borough Station, and the date is 29th June 1952. J.C.Gillham

The request version of the LUT/MET design is shown here on Great Dover Street. Notice that it is fitted to one of the Southwark Council lamp posts. J.C.Gillham

The compulsory stop version of the first LPTB type is seen on Southwark Bridge Road at Glenham Street. The words – LONDON and TRANSPORT – are separated by the blue TRAMWAYS bar. J.C.Gillham

We progress to the second LPTB type. This has dropped the full legend TRAMWAYS in favour of the shortened form: TRAM. J.C.Gillham

We observe the third, and final, LT type in Lee High Road. The standard white roundel is on a medium blue field, and these colours were reversed for the compulsory stop version. J.C.Gillham

This design of concrete post with timetable panel is very familiar to Londoners, but only a few were used for tram stops. Here on the Embankment, we note the slots for route numbers 33 and 35, another uncommon feature for trams. J.C.Gillham

APPENDIX

SELECTED BIBLIOGRAPHY

No seeker after knowledge about London's tramways should be without a copy of Stan Collins' book *The Wheels Used To Talk To Us*, published by Sheaf Publishing in 1977. Other knowledgeable volumes written by former employees are *Bare Empty Sheds* by G. Harry Guilmartin, published by the Tramway & Light Railway Society in 1986, and *London Tramway Memories* by Harry Ellis, published by the LRTL in 1975.

John Reed's *London Tramways*, published by Capital Transport in 1997, gives a good overview of tramway operation 1861–1952. Two volumes by Julian Thompson entitled *London Trams In Camera*, published by Ian Allan in 1971, and *London's Trams*, published by Ian Allan in 1992, are packed with facts about the last years of the system. Another work dealing with the final conversion stages is *Operation Tramaway* by J. Joyce, published by Ian Allan in 1987.

Unfortunately, when the trams were running there was very little in the way of helpful literature, however, two enthusiasts' guides give a genuine flavour of the era. *ABC London's Transport . . . Trams and Trolleybuses* by S. L. Poole was published by Ian Allan in 1948. An even earlier volume is that written by the splendidly named Barrington Tatford in 1944; it too was published by Ian Allan, under the title *ABC London Transport Services*. Detailed photographic coverage of London's tramway routes is available in the 25 metropolitan volumes of the *Tramway Classics* series, published by Middleton Press and edited by the present author.

The chapter on the campaign to save the trams was helped by Ann Watkins' unpublished account of the work of Alan Watkins. A good series of articles on the background to the conversion programme 1931–1952 is contained in *Tramway London*, edited by Martin Higginson and published by the LRTA in 1993.

The large scale map series drawn by Frank Merton Atkins is very useful in determining track layouts right up to the final abandonment. Sadly the sheets on the metropolitan area were never completed, but photocopies can still be obtained from the John Price Memorial Library at the National Tramway Museum.

Information on the bus side of the London tramway conversions is readily available in Ken Glazier's book *Routes to Recovery*, published by Capital Transport in December 2000. Articles by Ken Glazier on the fortunes of London Transport's road services covering individual years 1949 to 1952 have appeared in various issues of the *London Bus Magazine*, published by the London Omnibus Traction Society. Many useful facts were also gleaned from the monthly magazine *Modern Tramway*, published by the Light Railway Transport League.

The official voice of London Transport was the monthly *London Transport Magazine* which contained all manner of articles and interviews covering both the traffic and the social side of a vast organisation. More recommended background reading comes in the form of *London from the bus top* by Lucy Masterman, published by Dennis Dobson in 1951, and *South London* by Harry Williams, published by Robert Hale in 1949.

Top On Saturday 21st October 1950, the noontime rush is in full swing at Tooting Broadway. The motorman of car 1787 is no doubt keeping one eye open for the many cyclists, whilst at the same time awaiting the green light, so that he can emerge from Upper Tooting Road. The following Feltham is probably working service 8 and will turn to the right of the picture into Mitcham Road.

Bottom Bus route 45 has already taken over from tram route 34 in this view of Stockwell Road, Brixton. Electric traction is still present in the shape of car 195 working service 78 from West Norwood to Victoria.